THE
SALMON RIVERS OF SCOTLAND

BY

AUGUSTUS GRIMBLE

IN four volumes, which will be similar in size and get-up to the *éditions de luxe* of " Deerstalking," " Shooting and Salmon Fishing," " Highland Sport," and " Deer Forests of Scotland." Each volume will contain from thirty to forty illustrations, together with a map of the rivers described; the greater part of them from the author's personal knowledge and from information gathered from owners, renters, their employees, and anglers in general. The rivers will be taken in order, and thus anyone will be able to see at a glance the following details :—

1. Course—length and characteristics from the angler's point of view.

2. The marches and extent of each fishery.

3. Positions of fords, foot and carriage bridges.

4. Duration of net and rod season and the best months for salmon and grilse.

5. Length of rod required and regulations as to use of gaff and landing net.

6. The right size and patterns of flies to use, and dressings of any special local ones.

7. How each fishery is let and to whom to apply.

8. Lures, other than the fly, that may be used with advantage on rivers where bait fishing is recognised.

9. Names and addresses of head fishermen on well-known reaches.

10. The numbers and names of all pools on each water, the length of time required to fish it, and notes on any pools requiring special casting.

11. Whether trousers, stockings, or neither are required.

12. The number of nets at the mouth, with names and addresses of owners and renters.

13. Most suitable weather, best size of water, and how long remaining in order after a flood.

14. Various ways of packing fish and some hints thereon.

15. Record catches and remarkable angling incidents.

16. Average take to rod and net, and average size of salmon and grilse.

17. Sea trout flies and sizes.

18. Mention of historical, traditional and legendary events not generally known, that have taken place on the banks of rivers.

Volume I. will contain some remarks on the 1898 Report, issued by the Fishery Board of Scotland on "Investigations of the Life History of .Salmon"; some remarks on Salmon Marking, and on Hatcheries.

Volume II. will contain a chapter on "Netting—Legal and Illegal," and Pollutions.

Volume III. will contain a chapter on "Poaching and its Prevention."

Volume IV., one on Rivers capable of improvements, with suggestions for carrying them out and thereby increasing the supply of salmon for food and sport, and augmenting alike the value of net and rod fishing.

The subscription for the set of the four books is £10 10s., but single copies can be subscribed for *pro rata*. Orders may be sent to any bookseller or the publishers, KEGAN PAUL, TRENCH, TRÜBNER & Co., Ltd., Paternoster House, Charing Cross Road.

November, 1899.

TABLE OF REFERENCE

THE SALMON RIVERS

OF

SCOTLAND

THE SALMON RIVERS

OF

SCOTLAND

BY

AUGUSTUS GRIMBLE

AUTHOR OF

"DEERSTALKING," "SHOOTING AND SALMON FISHING,"
"HIGHLAND SPORT," "THE DEER FORESTS OF SCOTLAND,"
"LEAVES FROM A GAME BOOK."

VOLUME I.

LONDON
KEGAN PAUL, TRENCH, TRÜBNER & CO.
LIMITED
PATERNOSTER HOUSE, CHARING CROSS ROAD, W.C.
1899

LONDON:
PRINTED BY WILLIAM CLOWES AND SONS, LIMI
STAMFORD STREET AND CHARING CROSS.

𝔇𝔢𝔡𝔦𝔠𝔞𝔱𝔢𝔡

BY PERMISSION,

WITH THE GREATEST RESPECT,

TO

OUR PREMIER ANGLER,

HIS ROYAL HIGHNESS THE DUKE OF YORK.

THE SALMON RIVERS OF SCOTLAND.

VOL. I.

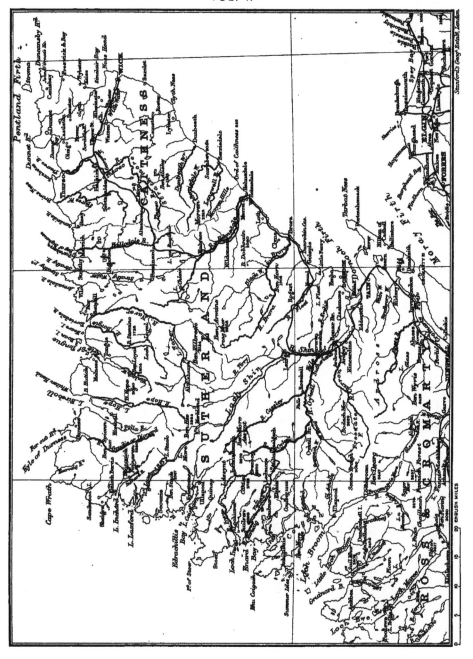

TABLE OF REFERENCE

LIST OF CONTENTS

LIST OF FULL-PAGE ILLUSTRATIONS

———•———

LIST OF ILLUSTRATIONS IN TEXT

PREFACE

———•———

" IF you have run one salmon you have run all
salmon !" thus, when noticing my book of " Shooting
and Salmon Fishing," wrote the critic of a journal
devoted entirely to sport. Good heavens ! what an
utter lack of enthusiasm, appreciation and observation must have possessed him !

But anglers who have killed many salmon with
the fly never talk of " running " them—the king of
fishes is " risen," " hooked " and " played," and it is
only the pike fisher who has his " runs " ; the use of
the expression points, therefore, to the probability
that my kind critic, for he evidently meant to be
very nice, was more conversant with that sport than
with salmon catching. But be that as it may, I
now live in fear lest a notice of these books should

commence by saying, " If you have seen one salmon river you have seen all salmon rivers ! "

But, kind reader, pray believe nothing of the sort, for it is not the fact ; and in trying to prove it my chief fear is that I shall not be able to do full justice to the subject, or have sufficient command of language to convince you that, just as every fish hooked, played, and lost or landed differs in its behaviour from all former ones and from all that may happily follow, so likewise every fresh river visited and cast over by an angler presents some fresh features not previously seen in others, or to be met with again in the new waters of the future.

In compiling these volumes I have availed myself of all information which was fairly at my disposal, my warmest thanks being due to the numerous gentlemen who have done all in their power to help me. To the best of my knowledge I have been in communication with every salmon river owner or renter of angling in Scotland, and have met with nothing but kindness, and in many cases offers of sport and hospitality. One or two proprietors were at first alarmed lest I was writing in the interest of the tourist angler, for though amongst that numerous body I have met many right good gentlemen and right good fishers, I have also came across others—thank goodness a small minority—who have fairly earned a bad name for themselves. These are the "'Arrys" who wander off into deer forests and grouse moors, disturbing large tracts of country while they seek some burn or loch they have heard well spoken of, but on which they have no right to fish; and on the banks they leave unpleasant souvenirs of their visits in the shape of lunch papers and perhaps small heaps of broken bottles for good dogs to gallop over! Then, again, there are those who ask right and left for a day's salmon fishing from perfect strangers and grumble furiously if they are refused.

In some parts of Scotland which are more

tourist overrun than others, these applications are so incessant and so numerous as to become a perfect pest, and if one quarter of the " permits " asked for were granted it would not leave a clear day a week for the owner himself. One gentleman I know was at last reduced—much against the innate courtesy of his nature—to treating these numerous requests with silent neglect. This had the desired effect, for it soon got known, and thus a nuisance which had lasted for years was at last stopped.

There are several distinct advantages to be claimed for salmon fishing, as against stalking and shooting—the angler on perfectly strange waters need not be entirely in the hands of the forester or the ghillie, as the would-be deer-slayer is with his stalker, whilst it is on the angler himself that the hardest part of the day's work falls, for if he be keen he will have to thrash away hour after hour while his ghillie may be seated comfortably on the bank smoking his pipe. Deer, too, may be wounded and escape—a most unpleasant matter to reflect on when the excitement of the day is over —but there is no such thing as a wounded fish; true, it may have gone off with the fly in its mouth or stuck in some other part of its body; nevertheless, it is always regarded as a lucky fellow—fit subject, perhaps, for a mild anathema, but never to be pitied.

Then there is often a limit placed on the number of deer to be killed in a day, but such a thing as a limit on the number of fish to be caught has never been heard of. With all these little points taken into consideration, and having regard to the pleasures of anticipation and uncertainty and the happy memories of realisation, it will be seen that the salmon fisher has as much, if not more fun than the deerstalker.

For several years past there has been a steady decline in the number of fish caught by nets and rods, and this season of 1899 has been the

very worst on record as far as it has gone.* In
the following chapters various suggestions for improving the Salmon Fisheries are put forward with
great diffidence. First and foremost it seems to me
that in cases where all the coast netting rights
and the whole of both banks of a river belong
entirely to one proprietor, it is not sufficiently
realised what large sums are lost by not taking
full advantage of such a happy position. I am not,
however, writing entirely on behalf of the rod, and
readily recognise that any question involving a
"food supply" should take precedence of mere
sport, however dearly anglers may be prepared
to pay for it. I do contend, however, that
continuously good netting times must also be continuously good angling times, and that if the take
of salmon by nets can be largely increased, that
then the take of salmon by rods must inevitably
follow suit.

* 1st June, 1899.

It always makes me laugh to hear our M.P.s talking grandly about salmon as a "food supply," a term that surely means some article of food brought within reach of all; and certainly, for the last forty years, salmon has never been at such a price as would bring it within reach of the working classes. A pound of salmon has ever been dearer than a pound of mutton. The ordinary net renter works only with the object of filling his pocket, and as long as he can sell his catch at a price that will give him a good profit, one cannot expect him to trouble himself about salmon as a food supply in the true acceptation of the term.

How this increased supply is to be brought about is eminently a question that should be dealt with by Parliament, and if the stricter enforcement of the existing laws, or the making of any simple new ones, can reduce the retail price of salmon in May from 3s. 6d. per lb. (that is the price as I write) to 8d. or 6d., then our law-makers should at once set to work to bring about such a desirable and popular state of affairs.

In these volumes I have humbly endeavoured to show how easily salmon might be brought within the reach of all, and if my readers will honour me by perusing, in Volume I., the chapter on "The Life History of the Salmon," on "Salmon Marking," and on "Hatcheries"; in Volume II. that on "Netting, Legal and Illegal," and on "Pollutions"; in Volume III. the one on "Poaching and its Prevention"; and in Volume IV. "Rivers Capable of Improvement," in which chapters I humbly venture to put forward some theories of my own, together with the condensed opinions of many cleverer heads than mine, they will, I trust, be convinced of the feasibility of some of the schemes advocated.

The matter is not one in which the voice of the tacksman should be too much considered, it is the same to him whether he nets one fish of twenty pounds and sells it at Billingsgate for half-

a-crown a pound, or whether he takes five fish of
the same weight and sells them there at sixpence
a pound ; in either case he receives fifty shillings,
and it is probable that he would prefer to see the
price kept high.

The excessive multiplication of bag nets and
their more scientific working, coupled in very
numerous cases with the non-observance of the
weekly close time, are doubtlessly reducing the
salmon, and it is from Parliament and not from net
owners or renters that the public should demand
cheap salmon. In a few years that could easily be
made a certainty by placing a limit on the number
of bag nets per mile of coast; by such a strict
supervision of these nets as would prevent them
from habitually disregarding the weekly close time,
by revising the estuary limits, by abolishing bag nets
working between the mouths of rivers only a few
miles apart (as for instance Dee and Don), by an
extension of the weekly or annual close time, by
establishing severer and more efficacious methods

of punishing the wholesale poaching by scringing. If these matters were taken in hand earnestly, four years after the good work was commenced a dinner of spring salmon would be within reach of every working man in the kingdom, and then, when the price was so small, those who now pay five shillings a pound for February salmon would begin to wonder how they could ever have been so foolish.

In conclusion, I wish to thank the many kind friends who have at various times given me salmon fishing ; especially Sir William Cunliffe Brooks, Charles Chetwode Baily, Captain G. W. Hunt, Colonel Murray of Polmaise, and E. Brydges Willyams, to whose kindness I am indebted for many happy rod-in-hand days on such fine waters as those of Glen Tana and Park on the Dee, the Dupplin Water of the Earn, the Breadalbane Water of the Awe, the Waster Elchies beat of the Spey, and the Langwell stretch of the Oykel ; to them and all other fishing friends I wish tight lines, and if anything in these pages leads to the greater frequency of that longed-for moment the hard work of putting them together will be amply rewarded.

And now to make my salaam to my subscribers, and trusting that nothing I have said has annoyed either owner or renter of either netting or angling, I will honestly confess that the writing of these four volumes has proved a far heavier undertaking than I estimated at the outset, and having said that much, I will bring this somewhat lengthy preface to an end.

A. G.

UNION CLUB, BRIGHTON,
31*st May*, 1899.

THE

SALMON RIVERS OF SCOTLAND.

Chapter I.

THE ALNESS

Rises in Mr. Walter Shoolbred's Forest of Kilder-
morie, flows into Loch Morie, which is partly in the
forest, and on leaving it enters the Novar property.
There are, however, no salmon in Mr. Shoolbred's
part of the river, as the fish do not reach Loch
Morie; nevertheless, he maintains a hatchery capable
of taking 80,000 ova; in addition to this the Alness
District Board have another one on the lower
reaches capable of turning out 100,000 fry.

After leaving Loch Morie the Alness has a
rapid, rocky run of some fifteen miles, until it falls

into the Cromarty Firth a little below the pretty village of Alness.

The angling is divided amongst the four lower proprietors, Ardross and Novar having by far the largest portion ; the mile nearest the sea goes with Major Mackenzie's property of Dalemore and that of Teaninich, which he also rents. Then on the left bank Mr. Dyson Perrins' Ardross Castle estate comes in, while on the right Novar and Teaninich have the rest of the river; the four proprietors preserving their fishings strictly, and uniting to protect and improve them.

The river opens on the 11th of February, the Cromarty Firth nets come off on the 26th of August, and the rod continues till the 31st of October. Though clean fish are got in the nets of the Firth at the opening of the season, the Alness itself is of no use until the first flood after the middle of June, and then salmon, grilse, and sea trout (fast becoming extinct) all ascend together. There are neither cruives, obstructions, pollutions, or disease, while the upper reaches have excellent spawning grounds. A fourteen-foot rod will be ample—indeed a trout rod will suffice, and when fishing this stream some twenty years ago I used nothing else, taking care to have fifty yards of reel line and good stout salmon gut, the last strand or two next the fly being somewhat finer than the whole line.

The fish run from seven to ten pounds, although each season some are got which scale from fifteen to twenty. Any of the small standard patterns will kill; perhaps the best are the Doctors, Jock Scot, and Childers. No waders are wanted, and the fly is the only lure used. The river rises and falls with such great quickness that only those residing on the spot have any chance of sport.

One of the proprietors writes :—" I am sorry to think our Highland rivers are going from bad to worse; indeed, unless united action is taken all over Scotland for the better protection of salmon and the establishment of hatcheries, our rivers will

soon not be worth fishing. Poor as it has been,
angling has yet added materially to the value of
the shooting rents, and if the fishing is allowed to
fall away to nothing, surely the shooting rents will
fall also, and therefore it is to the interests of all
proprietors to take the matter up earnestly."

This sensible letter only confirms the plain-
spoken Report made by the Clerk to the Alness
District Board to the Fishery Board for Scotland,
and though dated as far back as 1895 and repeated
in each succeeding Report, no steps have been
taken by the Fishery Board for Scotland to remedy
the evils so graphically described.

Thus as follows writes the Clerk to the Alness
Board :—"The systematic and wholesale poaching
in the Cromarty Firth, by fishermen from Cromarty, is causing much loss.   Last spring six boat
crews (thirty men) were engaged in fishing for sea
trout in the Cromarty Firth, inside the Sutors of
Cromarty, with sweep or trawl nets about 200
yards long and with small meshes.   They fish in

much the same way as salmon fishers do, shooting out their nets and hauling them on the beach. They pretend to be fishing for flounders and other white fish, but it is well known that but for the sea trout they could not make anything of this mode of fishing. In consequence of the system of watching maintained by the Local Board this mode of fishing is now chiefly carried on at night, but the Board are practically powerless to suppress it then, as the fishermen are in great force, resist apprehension, can seldom be identified, and the sea trout are got rid of before a capture can be made. The Board have for some years been incurring an expenditure which involves a very heavy tax on the owners of salmon fishings in the district, in order to suppress this destructive and illegal fishing, but for the reasons referred to have only met with limited success. Unless the Fishery Board takes steps to prevent trawling of this kind there is grave reason to fear that the Alness will by-and-by cease to be a sea trout river."

A strong and clear statement like the foregoing,
but published only in a Fishery Board Report,
is not likely to be seen by either land or water
thieves—the former, however, are very fully aware
that the land police are an unfortunate fact, that
they are capable and powerful, and able to deal
with any land poaching. The water thieves, on the
contrary, know from experience that the water
police are incapable of preventing water poaching,
and know that though they cannot defy and jeer
at the laws while on land, yet, when they are on
the water, as matters are at present, they can treat
the law with contempt.

There is only one other salmon river flowing
into the Cromarty Firth—the Conon. Perhaps if the
proprietors of the two rivers combined together to
suppress this poaching and to rent the Firth nets,
and work them only long enough to recoup them
their outlay, and pay six per cent. on the money
invested, the angling of both rivers might be greatly
improved. Good angling means the certainty of

letting it for a big rent, or the certainty of great sport if the angling be kept by the owner. Of course he cannot eat his cake and have it, but in either case the increased profit or increased sport will pay a great deal better than the profit

ARDROSS CASTLE.

foregone on the netting after expenses and interest have been earned.

In the case of the Alness and the Conon, it is the latter river that would derive by far the larger share of the benefits, but that is a matter that

should be easily arranged amongst the different
proprietors of the two streams.

Prior to the purchase of Ardross by Mr. Dyson
Perrins, this beautiful place was rented by Sir
Greville Smyth.   During that time his brother-in-
law, Colonel Way, while fishing near the castle,
caught a salmon of some nine pounds, which he at
once carried up to the small loch in the grounds
and turned it in.   There it lived for two years, in
the meanwhile daily growing blacker and thinner,
until it died ; one more proof that a land-locked
river salmon cannot exist for very long in fresh
water, even though there be a constant stream
passing through, as there was in this case.

Chapter II.

THE BERRIEDALE AND LANGWELL.

These two Caithness streams, draining an area of seventy-two square miles, are best dealt with together, as at some two hundred yards from the sea they unite at Berriedale, after flowing entirely through the Duke of Portland's deer forest. The Berriedale, the more northern of the two, has a run of about twenty miles, which is just double the length of the Langwell, and the larger river holds slightly heavier and earlier fish, for clean ones have been taken on the 7th of March, while one of twenty-five pounds is the top weight ever landed by the rod. The fish of the two streams are easily distinguishable, and each breed keeps strictly to its own river.

It requires from eight to twelve hours' rain to put these waters into good ply, while a twenty-four hours' drought brings them, as far as sport goes, nearly as suddenly to a standstill, and in neither is there any angling until some distance up from the sea.

On the Berriedale the best killers are the Childers, Jock Scot, and silver-bodied flies of sizes ranging from one-and-a-half to seven of Limerick hooks. A fourteen-foot rod is of ample length, and both rivers can be fished without waders. With regard to the nicest kind of rod for use on small rivers in which fish seldom exceed ten pounds, I have found it pleasanter to use a rather stout eleven-foot trout rod. There is hardly any labour in casting, and the fly can be placed to an inch, and also delivered more neatly than with a two-handed rod. The fish when hooked has not water enough in these small streams to get more than twenty or thirty yards away, and though it will take a few minutes more to kill, that is of no great consequence. With this

sort of rod no treble gut is required ; the salmon gut
is attached direct to the reel-line, the same as if
fishing for trout.

In neither of these streams are there many sea
trout ; June, July and August are best for salmon
and grilse, but unless the angler is a resident at
Berriedale and prepared to take advantage of every
rainfall, the chances of sport are not great during
these months, which are usually dry ones. There
are no pollutions or serious obstacles to the passage
of fish, though about ten miles up the Berriedale
there is a fall which they cannot pass in times of
drought.

The season for nets is from the 11th of
February to the 26th of August, but the rod may
be plied till the 31st of October. The Duke's
keepers do all the protection, but I was not able
to ascertain whether they ever visited the sea nets
before 6 A.M. on Monday mornings and made sure
that the weekly close time had been observed and
the leads duly removed. With reference to the

non-observance of the weekly close time by the
sea nets, I wish to refer my readers for fuller
information with regard to all nets to my
chapter on "Netting, Legal and Illegal," in
Vol. II.

When these streams are "right" each will give
two or three fish a day to the rod. Lord Charles
Bentinck had five one day and on another occasion
Miss Chandos Pole had four from the Rock Pool
of the Berriedale. On the Langwell the best fishing is from a little above McEwan's, the Head
Forester's, Cottage, some five miles from the sea,
down to the Langwell Kitchen Gardens, a stretch
of about three miles in which there are many
pretty little pools. Salmon run from five to eight
pounds and grilse from three to five, and about
fifty fish a season are got from each river. The
same flies that kill on the Berriedale are also
good for the Langwell, but in addition there is a
local fly called "The Stalker," with which the
Duke got six fish one day.

The dressing is as follows:

Tag : Silver twist and turn of yellow floss silk.

Tail : Golden pheasant rump feather.

Body : Darkish green mohair, silver twist or tinsel.

At Shoulder : Claret hackle with jay over.

Wing : Brown turkey, small jungle cock cheeks, and two strands of blue macaw.

These rivers run into the sea through a bar of gravel, which, according to the Fishery Board Report of 1884, completely closes the access in times of drought. Gravel bars are, however, shifting affairs, and I am glad to say that when I saw it on the 9th of June this year, although there had been no rain for three weeks, there was just sufficient water coming through to let fish pass up as the tide rose.

The five or six bag-nets at the mouth of these two streams belong to Mrs. Dunbar, the widow of a son of the late John Dunbar, of Thurso fame, and under the guidance of Angus Henderson,

kindly deputed to show me all he could by
Mr. King, the Duke's factor at Berriedale, on
visiting these nets I received an invitation from
the head man—one Adam Macpherson—to proceed
to sea with him and his men and visit the nets, a

MENDING A BAG-NET AT THE MOUTH OF THE BERRIEDALE
AND LANGWELL RIVERS.

chance of which I gladly availed myself; but on
this occasion, although they had not been looked at
for nearly twelve hours, they were all empty, a
fact for which Adam blamed the cloudless sky
and the clear still water.

These bag-nets, by some curious clause of the
existing Estuary Bye-Laws, are fishing nearer to
the mouth of these rivers than is usual, or indeed
lawful, in other places.   None of them were over
four hundred yards from the mouth, two of them
were certainly within two hundred yards—in fact
I judged the distance at one hundred yards, but
to make all certain I have named the longer one,
as judging distance across water is apt to be
deceptive ; be this as it may, certain it is that nets
fishing in such unusually close proximity to the
mouth of two rivers must greatly reduce the
numbers of fish that would ascend them, and both
have good spawning grounds.

The same report of the Fishery Board already
mentioned states later on that " from six to eight
thousand fish, chiefly grilse, are annually taken in
this *District*," a somewhat puzzling statement, as
only a few lines before it is expressly set forth
that there is " not a single District Board in the
County of Caithness."   Probably the description is

intended to apply to the united bag-nets fishing
the mouths of the two rivers under discussion, and
the rest of the eight miles of coast up to and
north of the Dunbeath River.

During my stroll up the beautifully wooded
banks of the Langwell, we met a ghillie exercising
a fine team of black and white pointers, the wild
deer feeding in the grassy strath below taking no
notice of them. On reaching the head keeper's
house, a little further up the glen, we found some
fifteen stags, with horns about three parts grown,
and, of course, still in velvet, lying on a grass plat
in front of the kennels, and it was indeed an odd
sight to see the keeper unbolt a door and let loose
upwards of a dozen fine deerhounds. Out they
dashed, bounding about in all directions, full in
sight of the deer. Then a word from the keeper
sent them all off into another grass field, the deer
meanwhile hardly troubling to move. From here
I was taken to the splendidly placed house of
Langwell, with its wonderful sea view; and

arrived there, a charming old housekeeper invited
me inside. And now, if I had the pen of "The
World" correspondent, who writes those amusing
articles "Celebrities at Home," I could have
written a long letter on "The Duke of Portland
at Home." Suffice it, however, to say that of the
many pretty things I saw, that which interested
me most was a well set-up salmon of 62 lbs.!
hauled ashore by Adam Macpherson from the
Berriedale nets in June, 1894. Length, 51$\frac{5}{8}$ inches;
girth, 29$\frac{3}{4}$ inches. A magnificent specimen, which
no angler could set eyes on without feeling a
burning desire for a chance of trying conclusions
with a similar one. This big fish could hardly
have wished to ascend either the Berriedale or the
Langwell. Macpherson thinks he was a Norway
giant that had lost his way; more probably, however, it was a Tay fish who had struck the shore
very far north of his own river.

Close to this "sockdollager" there was a finely
shaped fish of exactly half the size, taken by the

Duke on the 28th of April, 1897, from the English-woman's Pool of the Garry of Loch Oich.   Near this were two interesting specimens of natural history, one in the shape of a bee-eater, in fine plumage, killed in Langwell Gardens; the other being a pole-cat, now so nearly extinct in Scotland. Then came the billiard-room, a glorious sight to the eyes of any deerstalker, for on the walls hang a splendid collection of Langwell Forest heads, amongst which are many curious malformations; and here I could have lingered for several hours, but time was up, the trap was waiting, the sun setting, and the Ord of Caithness had to be negotiated, so with reluctance I came to the end of a day passed, thanks to His Grace's kindness, in one of the most beautiful and well-kept places in the kingdom.

Chapter III.

THE BORGIE.

THE total length of this pretty stream, in which disease has not at present made an appearance, is twenty - one miles, inclusive of the four lochs through which it flows. Draining an area of sixty-two square miles, it rises some six miles to the north of Altnaharra. After a short run its head streams flow into the narrow loch of Coulside, and issuing from thence in a little more than a mile they expand into Loch Laoghoal, or Loyal, which is some five miles long, and united by short narrows first to Loch Craggie and then to Loch Slam. On leaving this last-named loch the river has a further run of nine-and-a-half miles before it falls into the sea at Torrisdale Bay, about a mile to the west of

Navermouth.   On this lower reach of the Borgie
there is one considerable fall, which fish do not
ascend before the middle of April ; but after that
date salmon and grilse are occasionally caught in
Loch Slam, less frequently on Loch Craggie, and
very rarely in Loch Laoghoal, and then only by
trolling.   The angling has greatly fallen off, for
twenty years ago as many as seven fish have been
got in Loch Slam in one day, while now that is
about the take of the whole season, although the
loch is much more regularly fished for salmon than
in the old times.   The fishing of the river goes
with the Borgie shootings, and opening on the 11th
of January for the rod, it may be fished until the
30th of September.   The nets may not begin to
work till the 11th of February, and have to stop
on the 26th of August.   No wading is necessary,
and the river can easily be fished with a grilse rod.
February and March are the chief months for
salmon, the best lures being Jock Scot, Childers,
Popham and Yellow Eagle, sizes from 3/0 to No. 6.

Grilse run in June and July, and are more partial to the charms of small silver or black bodied flies, while sea trout, which are very scarce, affect the Zulu. In low water the worm kills well, but except on occasions when a fish is badly wanted it is rarely used. The yearly average take is seventy salmon and grilse, the former scaling ten pounds and the latter five.

Between Loch Slam and the sea there are some twenty casts, the best of which are perhaps "The Long Pool," "Brecku," "Black Bank," and "The Fall Pool." At present the mouth of the Borgie is worked by a net and coble, which is in the hands of the same syndicate of gentlemen that have the netting and angling of the Naver, and they do not begin work till May. Of late years there have been no very good takes to the rod, and three fish is now considered excellent, although in 1889–1891 six a day were common.

Late in the season the fish push their way right up into the stream falling into the head of Loch

Coulside, where they spawn in good numbers, but
as the parr or the smolts hatched there have to
run the gauntlet of four lochs, each holding hungry
brown trout, it is only to be expected that their
numbers will be considerably reduced by the time
they reach the sea, though perhaps not more so
than if they had to descend twenty miles of a river
equally well stocked with their natural destroyers.

Some years ago, from the middle of April, a
few salmon used to be got in Loch Laoghoal by
trolling, and at that time there were also plenty
of Ferox in this loch, which now appear to have
died out, as in recent years hardly one has been
caught. All these four lochs in connection with
the Borgie are open to the public staying at
Altnaharra or Tongue Hotels, and are *very* hard
fished, while but little is done in the matter of
restocking, and the incessant taking out and
putting nothing in must sooner or later tell a tale
of deterioration. It should, however, be mentioned
that in all the inns on the Sutherland property

there is hung up in a prominent place a request
that anglers shall return to the water all trout
under eight inches, a matter which on the whole
is fairly well observed.

The Fishery Board Report of 1889 states that
in the "Tongue District" (there is no such
"District" named on their "Map of Districts" of
1894), which I take it includes the Hope, Kinloch,
Borgie, Naver, and perhaps Halladale, the take of
salmon has steadily decreased for the last three
years.

The yield for 1888 of these five rivers and
their coasts having been 1,817 salmon, weighing
21,161 lbs., or nearly a twelve pound average, and
9,977 grilse of 52,409 lbs., or over five pound
average, and next follows a mention of a beggarly
199 sea trout of 330 lbs. As against this 11,794
fish, the Report then states that the rods of these
six rivers killed 300 fish as their share. Surely a
most disproportionate allowance! but there it is in
black and white, and the accuracy of Fishery

Board Reports cannot be doubted. In the above return the enormous difference in the take of salmon and grilse cannot fail to be noticed. Five-and-a-half babies are killed to every adult ! Surely that cannot be the right way to bring about an increase of any population ?

The 1889 Report further states that, " The Bye-laws with regard to the observance of the weekly and *annual* close time are not very strictly observed by the bag-nets." I can only say from personal observation that this remark is *not half strong enough*, for there are certainly several hundreds of bag-nets that throughout the whole season *entirely* disregard the law as to the weekly close time.*

Mr. John Box, the Duke of Sutherland's factor at Tongue, who is fully qualified by long experience to speak with authority, has for many years advocated that netting in this district should cease on the 15th of August instead of on the 26th, by which

---

* See Vol. II., Chapter on " Netting, Legal and Illegal."

means many more grilse would be left to ascend
these rivers, and it is remarkable that nothing has
ever been done to give effect to these strong and
repeatedly expressed opinions.   This Borgie is one
of the rivers that I venture to think could be vastly
improved at a small cost, which would soon be
recouped by the increased value of both net and
rod fishing.*

When I visited it in June last a lengthy
drought had reduced it to a mass of stones, and
it was hardly possible to tell what it would be like
when full of water, but thanks to the kindness of
Mr. A. S. Bolton, of Moor Court, Oakamoor, who
now rents the Borgie shootings, his keeper, Hugh
Bruce, gave me much assistance, and that, coupled
with the valuable help of my old friend, Sir J.
Edwards-Moss, who rented Borgie for twelve years,
has enabled me to speak with confidence of this
pretty stream.

---

* See Vol. IV., Chapter on " Rivers Capable of Improvement."

The last-named gentleman writes me as follows :
"It is now some eight years since I wetted a line
on Borgie, and therefore I cannot speak with certainty. as to its present condition. The river is
doubtlessly one capable of great improvement.
About 1885 it fell away to almost *nil.* This was
in consequence of an abnormal August flood in
1883, when three distinct thunderstorms met and
burst about Ben Loyal. So heavy was the flood that
new channels were cut, and the whole bed of the
river torn up and altered and widened and thereby
shallowed. In 1887 Mr. Brereton, who then was
the Duke of Sutherland's factor, promised me £10
a year towards any improvements I cared to make,
and this was continued for two years, but withdrawn
on Mr. Brereton's resignation.

"In the meanwhile I had made certain quiet
resting-places for the fish, and the annual take
began to increase largely. These improvements
were chiefly effective in the early spring, as when
a spate came, bringing down a lot of ice, I believed

that fish were swept back to the sea for the want
of shelter, and the still, deep holes I made enabled
them to 'lie low' while the ice passed over their
heads. As long as I had Borgie these dams were
kept in good repair, but I understand that they
have now been destroyed by floods."

Chapter IV.

.THE BRORA

RISES to the north of Lairg; drains an area of one hundred and sixty-five square miles, and after a run of twenty expands into Loch Brora four miles long and nearly half a mile wide at the broadest part; issuing from the Loch, it runs another four miles and falls into the sea at Inver-brora. Opening on the 11th of February, it is usually well stocked with fresh-run fish on that date, and five, six, and seven fish a day are quite common events.

The whole course is through moorland country until it leaves the Loch, and then for half a mile, down to the Ford Pool, it flows through fir plantations, emerging again to banks of peat and heather until the sea is reached.

From time immemorial the Brora has been celebrated for the numbers of its salmon, and as far back as 1658 it is mentioned by Franck in his Northern Memoirs. Says he, "The next thing we meet with is the Lough Broroh that spurts forth a river into the bowels of the ocean. This Lough is deep, but not so large as the Ness, but very full of salmon, and though the river seems to have rapid streams, yet the tides influence them every twelve hours.* I mention this Broroh for no other purpose than to reflect on her plenty of salmon, where they barrel up for France and other parts annually (as reported) so much salmon as amounts to £300 sterling a year, and the price of a salmon (among themselves) seldom exceeds one single denare."

Later on, in 1813, Sir Humphrey Davy, in his "Salmonia," says: "The Brora is an admirable river. I have often rode over from the mansion

---

* In the present day the highest tide does not influence any stream that is over four hundred yards from the mouth.

of the princely and hospitable lord and lady of
that country after breakfast and returned at two
or three o'clock, having taken from three to eight
salmon—several times eight—and at that time I
should have placed the Brora above the Ewe for
certainty of sport."

In 1878 the Duke of Sutherland started a
hatchery, which was in some way not well or
scientifically managed, for the young fry died in
thousands in one of the burns into which they
had been turned out. So the experiment was dis-
continued, as the result of fry replaced in the river
did not in any way correspond with the numbers
of eggs taken from spawning fish—an unfortunate
result which is entirely at variance with the benefits
which have been derived elsewhere from other
hatcheries.

The Brora opens to rods and nets on the
11th of February, the netting season ending on the
26th of August, and that for the rod on the
31st of October; the river, however, might well be

made available for the rod on the 1st of February,
and closed to it on the 15th of October. I feel sure
such a step would be welcomed by the anglers,
while it would likewise be doing the river good
service.

For the early part of the season—up to the
end of March—an eighteen-foot rod will be wanted,
as the river usually runs big then, while its exposed
banks are visited almost daily by high winds, often
accompanied by snow storms. When April comes
and the water gets smaller, a rod of sixteen foot
will do all that is required, and then in May a
stout single-handed ten or eleven-foot trout rod will
suffice. The gaff is generally used and kelts drawn
ashore and returned uninjured.

In the early months flies are dressed on irons
ranging in Limerick sizes from 6/0 to 0, and later
on from No. 1 to the very smallest double-hooked
No. 11. Watson of Inverness dresses these latter
very neatly and inexpensively.

The fly is the only lure used, and all the

standard ones kill ; Jock Scot, Childers and the silver bodies for choice. There is also a good local fly invented by Donald Ross, who was keeper at Torrish on the Helmsdale for many years, but who has settled down to a farm on the banks of the Brora. Out of compliment to his old home he has christened it " The Torrish," and as it is a fine fly to look at, and a good killer, it is worth mention ; but it is best dressed on a big hook and used early in the season during the time of heavy water.

Tag : Silver twist—yellow floss.

Tail : Topping and gold pheasant ruff.

But : Black ostrich.

Body : Lower half silver twist, with yellow hackle where silver ends. Upper half dark yellow mohair, silver tinsel, and yellow hackle at shoulder.

Wing : Bronze turkey, strands of yellow and red, swan and teal, jungle-cock cheek, and ostrich head.

Wading trousers are necessary for high water

though when the river is at a medium height, all
the pools can be reached with stockings.

The river is fished by the respective occupiers

GORDONBUSH AND LOCH BRORA.

of Gordonbush, Balnakoil, and Sciberscross shootings.   Mr. F. C. Gunnis has had the first-named
pretty lodge, just six miles out of Brora, for fifteen
years, and to him I am indebted for my first cast

on the river, together with the bulk of the information given herewith. Balnakoil Lodge, three miles higher up than Gordonbush and just opposite Pol Feddar and a little below the Fall Pool of the Blackwater, divides the fishing right with Sciberscross, each taking three days a week. For several seasons Major Howey had Balnakoil and Mr. Hall Sciberscross, but the former gave up this spring, and now Mr. Hall is tenant of both places. The stretch from the Loch to the sea is fished by the two rods bank and bank about, and between them by the end of April they have often got four hundred fish in the eleven weeks. In the autumn, from the 1st of August, the tenant of Uppat Forest has the angling from the Loch to the sea for three or four days a week, the Duke of Sutherland keeping for himself the remaining days as may be arranged.

The first August floods bring sea trout into Loch Brora, but not in any great numbers. Whilst fishing for these with very small flies and

a light single-handed trout rod, Mrs. Gunnis
hooked and landed a nice salmon of ten pounds,
and Mr. Gunnis, on similar tackle, another of
eighteen pounds; and on this fine tackle, and with
the smallest double hooks, Mr. Gunnis lands a
good few fish every summer.

From the commencement of the season the fish
make at once for the Loch, and there they hang
about until the first week in March, when they
continue their upward course until they reach the
Fall Pool of the Blackwater. The Brora does
not hold many trout, and though there are a fair
quantity in the Loch, they are so gorged with
elvers that a fly has but little attraction for them.
The Loch is divided into three distinct sections,
united by narrows of sixty or seventy yards across.
Ten years ago it was very rare for salmon to be
got with the rod, but by dint of patient observation,
Mr. Gunnis has gained a knowledge of the places
they frequent, and every year he now kills some
fish in the Loch.

There are neither pollutions or obstructions,
and though disease has made its appearance at
intervals, it has never wrought very great havoc.
Spawning begins as early as the 10th of October
(a fact much in favour of opening the river for the
rod on the 1st of February or even the 11th of
January, the same as the Helmsdale, so close by),
and is finished by the end of November. Kelts
migrate about the middle of March, and have
departed by the middle of May, and then, in May
and June, the smolts go to the sea.

Three miles above Loch Brora the Blackwater
pours in its very considerable volume of water ;
indeed, from above the junction this tributary plays
a more important part than the River Brora itself,
for the bulk of the fish ascend this stream, and
but comparatively few pass up the Brora proper.
Immediately above the loch is about three-quarters
of a mile of dead water, into which, when the
river above is low, fish gather in great numbers,
and here, when there is a stiff breeze, they may

FALLS OF THE BLACKWATER

be taken with very small flies. In this way
Major Howey had seven one day, and on several
occasions Mr. Gunnis has had his half-dozen.
From the 1st of August Balnakoil and Gordonbush
divide this upper water between them, beat No. 1
being from the Fall Pool of the Blackwater down
to the Loch, and No. 2 extending from the top
of the Fall Pool for a considerable distance up the
Blackwater, in which the fish are beginning now to
get somewhat off colour. They ascend the Fall Pool
during the first week or so in May, and passing up
they enter a rocky gorge, in which there are many
good-looking casts ; but, strange to say, in this bit
of the water they seldom rise to the fly. Above
this gorge the river flows through a widish strath,
and here sport may confidently be expected.
Just before the Blackwater joins the Brora
is Pol Feddar, which, after the end of the
first week in March — depending on the size
of the water — is the best and largest of all
the pools : on the 3rd of March, 1894, Mr.

Gunnis had fish of 20 lb., 19 lb., 17 lb., and 7 lb. out of this pool.

With regard to the netting of the Brora, as far as the river itself is concerned, it could hardly be more leniently dealt with. The loch is netted five, six, or even seven times in the season up to the end of April, and as many as one hundred and wenty-five to one hundred and fifty fish have been taken in one haul. From the 1st of May only the Duke of Sutherland has two cobles and two nets working at the mouth from the picturesque "look-out." I had a long chat with the head man of these nets, who was much depressed at the bad fishing they were making this season, and was also most eloquent on the subject of the large numbers of salmon and grilse poached by the steam trawlers (see article "Poaching and its Prevention" in Vol. III.).

Leniently as the Brora mouth is treated, the netting of the whole coast is very severe, and unless curtailed must eventually tell, first, on

the sport of the Helmsdale and Brora, and then
on the quantity of the fish caught in the nets.
In the journey from Helmsdale to Brora anyone
can count from the train thirty-three bag nets,
several of them being double ones, extending one

THE LOOK-OUT AT BRORA MOUTH.

beyond the other into the sea. There are other
five nets visible a little to the north of Helmsdale
mouth, and between Brora and Golspie there are
twelve others, or fifty nets altogether (probably more,
as at times the sea coast is hidden from the eyes of

the railway traveller by the cuttings), let to Messrs.
Sellar, of Aberdeen.   These fifty nets are spread
over some sixteen miles of coast, and surely are
too numerous ; but for further remarks of cost,
equipment and maintenance, etc., see article on
" Netting, Legal and Illegal," in Vol. II.*

The following statistics, taken chiefly from the
fish book of Mr. Gunnis, will show the sport yielded
by this river of late years.

In 1891—fishing from the 30th of March to the
18th of April—Mr. Gunnis and Mr. E. Lort-Phillips
had eighty-four fish, seven of which came out
of the New Pool on the 3rd of April to the
rod of the last-named gentleman.   In the same
season, from the 20th of April to the 28th of
May, Mr. Gunnis, fishing alone, had another
sixty-two.

----

* See also Chapter on Improvements in Vol. IV., in which
I hope to be authorized to announce the removal of these
nets.

In 1892, from the 6th of April to the 2nd of
May, Mr. Gunnis and his guest, Mr. C. Darley,
had forty-nine fish.

In 1893, from the 3rd of March to the 18th of
April, Mr. Gunnis had one hundred and fifteen fish,
nearly the whole to his own rod.. In that season,
on the 21st of March, he had thirteen; on the
22nd of March, fourteen; and on the 23rd nine, or
thirty-six in the three days!

In 1895, Colonel Clifton had the Gordon Bush
rod (which is sometimes let when Mr. Gunnis is
in Somaliland), and from the 11th of February to
the 1st of April he got fifty fish.

In 1897, Mr. Gunnis got sixty fish from the 11th
of February to the 31st of March, and in April
and part of May Messrs. Brand, J. Head, Heywood
Thompson, and Major Hopwood had eighty-eight
fish.

In 1898, from the 11th of February to the
31st of March the water was let to Mr. A.
McCorquodale, who got just a hundred fish, the

largest being 24 lbs. ; while in April and May following Mr. Gunnis had ninety-seven others.

Twenty-nine pounds is the heaviest fish recorded to rod and line, and a forty-pounder to the Brora mouth net. But from the above statistics it will be seen that this river is a reliable one for sport—something will always depend on the skill and hard work of the angler, and on the state of the river. If, for instance, during March, the stones " should be coming up out of the watter," as the ghillie puts it, then, of course, sport must be greatly reduced. This, however, is not a very likely contingency, and I know of no stream that is more certain to give good sport in February and March than this one, while to anyone lucky enough to get a rod in it, there is the additional attraction of a very good hotel at Brora, not five minutes' walk from the lowest pool.

Most of the pools are fine big ones, easily fished, but requiring a long line in times of high water.

Below the Loch.

1. Otter Pool.	7. The Madman's.
2. The Ford.	8. The Cliff.
3. Fannich.	9. Bengies.
4. Rallan.	10. The Cruive.
5. The New Pool.	11. The Rock.
6. The Stream.	

Above the Loch.

1. Deadwater.	6. The Snag.
2. Dyke End.	7. The Flat.
3. Macdonalds.	8. Feddar.
4. The Round Pool.	9. The Stream.
5. Stocken.	10. The Fall.

Chapter V.

THE CASSELEY.

The Casseley—which is Gaelic for " the swift flood "—is another of the Kyle of Sutherland rivers, which, rising in the north-east slopes of Ben More, has a course of upwards of twenty miles, during which it drains seventy-five square miles of moor country before it falls into .brackish water at the pretty little village of Rosehall, just below the mouth of the Oykel and some eight miles above that of the Shin. About a mile up the river there is a steep fall, which blasting operations have rendered passable for fish, and again higher up there are similar obstructions recently dealt with in a like manner. Although, however, the lower falls are readily ascended, fish rarely pass up before the end of May or the first week in June. In

the mile or so of river lying below the Fall, fish
are occasionally got as early as the middle of
March, but April is the best month, although with
moist weather May is equally good; at all times,
however, rain is necessary, as the river runs down
very quickly. From the falls to the Kyle the
angling of the right bank belongs to Sir Charles
Ross, of Balnagowan, who lets it to Mr. W. E.
Gilmour, the owner of the Rosehall property and
the opposite bank. The combining of the two sides
has made a pretty bit of angling of an improving
sort, while it has put an end to the unpleasant
"racing" that formerly took place between the
occupants of the opposite banks. Since I fished
the Casseley with Mr. Gilmour in 1896, the upper
falls have also been blasted, and a great extent of
fresh spawning-ground opened up, and this, combined with the fact of the Casseley being a Kyle
of Sutherland river, leads me to prophesy with
some confidence a great improvement in sport.

The nets at the Kyle mouth and in the Dornoch Firth are now leased by a syndicate of gentlemen (Captain G. W. Hunt was the originator of the scheme and managed matters until ill-health compelled him to retire, and he is now worthily succeeded by the well-known Mr. H. H. Almond), whose avowed object is (after they have recouped themselves their expenses) to increase the supply of salmon and to improve sport; in this they will doubtlessly be backed up by the new proprietor of the lower Shin, Mr. Andrew Carnegie, of Skibo Castle. Therefore, I think I am right in advising anglers to secure fishing on any of these Kyle of Sutherland rivers.

The rod season is from the 11th of February to the 15th of October—the 30th of September would be better—the nets cease to ply on the 26th of August; but there are none nearer than Bonar Bridge. For their working I will refer my readers to the Chapter of "The Shin." The gaff is not permitted until the 1st of May, and as the banks offer but few gravelly places on which to strand a fish, a landing net is almost necessary.

Any of the medium-sized standard flies will kill—Jock Scot, Childers, and Black Doctor are the local favourites—and no other lure is permitted; waders are not required, and a grilse rod will easily cover all the water. The average yield of both banks of this pretty mile of water is thirty to thirty-five fish of ten pounds; it is sometimes let for the spring, and as there is no inn at Rosehall, anglers stay at the Post Office, where they are made very comfortable. There are but six casts in this lower beat: nearest the sea is the Bridge Pool, above that comes Little and Big Lazy Pool—both excellent chances; above them is the Round Pool, a pretty sure cast; then comes another pool, with a Gaelic name a great deal longer than the pool itself, and which I found wholly unpronounceable; and then the Fall Pool brings the angler to the top of the beat. Above the falls good sport is sometimes got if July be wet—the water there going with the Duchally property, rented for many years by Captain McTaggart, and owned by Mr. W. E. Gilmour

CHAPTER VI.

THE CARRON OF THE KYLE OF SUTHERLAND.

THE Carron rises in the Forest of Inverlael, drains
one hundred and twenty-two square miles, and,
after a course of twenty miles, all in Ross-shire,
falls into the Kyle of Sutherland, a little distance
west of Bonar Bridge station. The Blackwater
and the Calvie are the chief tributaries, and join
the main stream, the former on the north and the
latter on the south side, a little below Amat
House. It is a quick-running river, with plenty of
pretty pools and good spawning ground; but in the
earlier part of the season sport is entirely dependent
on rain or melting snow. It is easily fished,
and the paths from pool to pool on either bank

are well made and well kept up. The season opens on the 11th of February, closes for nets on the 26th of August, and for the rod on the 31st of October. The best months for salmon, which average 8 lbs., are March and April, and for grilse, average 5 lbs., from the middle of June to the end of August ; but sea trout are not plentiful.

On the lower reaches of Gledfield and Inver-charron an 18-feet rod may be used at the opening of the season, but a little later on one of sixteen feet will cover all the water with ease. The gaff is not prohibited, but kelts are always returned uninjured. The favourite flies, and they are the only lures used, are Jock Scot, Childers, and Sir Richard ; but any other standard pattern will kill if dressed on hooks ranging from 2/0 to the very smallest.

Wading trousers would be required if this river was fished in the usual way ; but it is understood between the opposite proprietors that the anglers on each bank shall confine their operations strictly to the pools that lie to the side of the water on which they are fishing—a very good arrangement, which it is to be regretted is not more universally adopted, for not only does it do away with the fatigue and unpleasantness of waders, but it also effectually stops any jealous racing for pools and the making of extra early risings so as to reach the river before the angler on the opposite bank.

By this arrangement, A, who has, say, the left bank, may be at work by 8 A.M. if he chooses, while B, who has the right bank, may breakfast at nine, smoke his pipe and write his letters at leisure, and then start for the river in the happy consciousness that the pools on his side have not been fished over by his more energetic neighbour.

Starting from the Kyle, the two miles nearest the sea on the right bank belong to Sir Kenneth Matheson, of Gledfield, and to his kindness I owe the pleasure of a long talk with old Lachlan

Monro, a hale and most sensible old keeper of
Sir Kenneth's, who has known the river for the
last fifty years, and when he first remembers it it
was easier to kill five or six fish in a day than
one now. This he puts down to the improvements

GLEDFIELD HOUSE.

in netting; in the forties most of it was done by
net and coble, and as in those days only shallow
nets were used, fishing could only be prosecuted at
half to low tide, and the fish had far better chances
of entering the river than they have with the deep

nets that now never cease working day and night,
"one out the other in."

Opposite Gledfield, about the first mile upwards
belongs to Mr. A. Littlejohn, of Invercharron, who
has the right of the net at Carron Mouth, a right
which for the last four seasons he has very liberally
abandoned in order to secure a better breeding
stock of fish and better sport. About two hundred
yards above Carron Bridge, on the left bank, the
Invercharron property ends, and Sir Charles Ross's
Braelangwell Reach begins and goes up for nearly
six miles.

These lower reaches of Gledfield and Invercharron are let occasionally, and for information on
this head it is best to write to McLeod, the inn-
keeper of the Balnagowan Arms at Bonar Bridge,
only a few yards from the station, and less than a
mile from the river, for it is at this comfortable
inn that the Carron anglers must stay. These
lower reaches fish best in March and April (the
15th of March to the 20th of April is the picked

time), and each should yield from twenty to twenty-five fish, although in this present unusually bad season the take has not been anything like as high as that. The best pools in these lower beats are :

The Boat Pool, nearest to the Kyle,

Jetty Pools,

Railway Bridge Pool,

Whirling Pool,

Raven or Rocky Pool, and hereabouts Invercharron water ends and Braelangwell begins and runs up for some six miles.

Then comes Gladfield Pool,

Little Fall,

Macgregors,

Mackenzies, and here the Gladfield water ends and the Countess of Cromartie's Dunie reach begins at the Dunie Burn. This fishing is rented by Mr. Littlejohn, who lets it with Invercharron. Following this is—

The Clump Pool,

Long Pool,

Hiding Pool,

Mrs. Ross' Pool, and then begins the Gruinard water, belonging to Mr. R. T. Coupland, which is some four miles in length, and holds the—

Corner Pool,

Lower and Upper Bulwark,

Ore's Pool,

Gruinard House Pool,

Stream Pool,

Moral,

The Keeper's Pool.

At the top of Braelangwell the Amat water, belonging to Mr. F. T. Gervers, commences, and here, after good heavy rain, plenty of fish may at times be killed, as many as twenty-two in a day having been taken by Colonel Long some thirty years ago. At the top of the Gruinard water Mr. W. Allis-Smith, of Glen Calvie, joins on, and here also in wet weather good fishing is to be had.

The Carron has neither obstructions, pollutions,

or disease, and is one of the four rivers—the Shin, Oykel, and Casseley being the other three— which will probably be altered for the better by the fact of the Bonar Bridge nets being in the hands of a syndicate of gentlemen, and further

THE CARRON FROM THE BRIDGE.

details of their objects will be found in the chapters relating to "The Shin." Suffice it to say that in 1897 all the Bonar Bridge nets were only worked five days a week, while during the latter part of the season they were only fished for sixty hours a

week. In my opinion, any one securing the lease
of a beat on any of these four rivers of the
Sutherland Kyle at the present price is pretty sure
of increased sport, or of being able to sub-let at a
higher rental.

CHAPTER VII.

THE DUNBEATH.

THIS small Caithness stream, which is wholly the property of Mr. W. S. Thomson-Sinclair, of Freswick, drains but twenty-three square miles of country, and from its source in the Dunbeath hill has but a twelve-mile run before it falls into the sea at Dunbeath, some six miles north of the Berriedale. The season is from the 11th of February to the 15th of October, nets coming off on the 26th of August. The best time for spring fish is from the middle of March to the middle of April, and these average about twelve pounds. It is, however, better for grilse and sea trout than salmon, July and August being the best months, and the average take is about fifty salmon and grilse.

There are bag nets on either side of the mouth, the right belonging to Mr. Thomson-Sinclair, and let to a tacksman. No wading is wanted—a small rod and small flies of the standard patterns are all that is necessary.

Chapter VIII.

THE DIONARD,

SOMETIMES called the Grudie of Durness, drains thirty-one square miles of very rocky high ground, and rising at the foot of one of the steep cliffs of Meal Horn in the forest of Gobernuisgach, after passing through two small lochs expands into Loch Dionard—a mile in length and a half broad; on leaving the loch it has a further run of fourteen miles before it falls into the Kyle of Durness, and as the descent averages as nearly as possible one hundred feet to the mile—for the loch is 1,380 feet above sea-level—the run is very rapid. The three tidal pools are jointly fished by the tenants of the Durness and Gualen Shootings and the Durness Hotel, the latter monopolising the lion's share.

Above these tidal pools the water of both banks, for four miles upwards, belongs to the Durness Shootings, for many years past rented by the late Mr. Brown, of Burghwallis Hall, Doncaster, who is now succeeded by his son.

About a mile above the bridge the Durness march ends, and from there upwards the rest of the river and Loch Dionard are entirely on the Gualen Shootings, the small Lodge of which (originally built by one of the late Dukes of Sutherland as a refuge for anyone travelling this desolate road in winter) is beautifully placed, directly facing the stony heights of Ben Spionnen, and, like Durness, it has had but one tenant for many years—Mr. C. E. Austen-Leigh.

The fly is the only lure used, and they range in size from $1\frac{1}{2}$ Limerick to the very smallest, the favourites being the genuine and the "blue" Jock Scot, the Green Highlander, the Doctor, and a local one called "The Brown Fancy," which is dressed as follows :

Tail: Two turns of silver twist and gold pheasant tipping.

Body: Brown mohair picked out at shoulder. Gold tinsel. Mallard wing.

The season is from the 11th of February to

DIONARD BRIDGE.

the 26th of August for nets, with extension to the rod until the 31st of October. A grilse rod will do all the work. No waders are required for Gualen, though perhaps on the lower reaches of Durness a pair of knee boots would be of advantage to anyone desirous of keeping perfectly dry.

On the Durness beat there are fifteen casts and some "bitties," the best being "the Wheel," "the Bridge," and "the Rock." Fish rarely come into the river before the end of June, but after that date they arrive with the first spate, and if it lasts long enough they at once go right up to Loch Dionard, where salmon, grilse, and sea trout may all be taken in August.

The Durness beat, if hard fished, will yield an average of forty salmon and grilse each season; the former averaging ten pounds and the latter five, while one of twenty-eight is the heaviest fish yet recorded. In August, 1896, Mr. Brown had two fairly good days in succession, the first giving six and the other five fish. In September this lower water at times holds a lot of sea trout, some having been caught of five pounds, though the average is one-and-a-half pounds, while from ten to twenty is reckoned a good day.

At the top of the Durness Reach the river
begins to alter in character, the scenery becoming
wilder, the stream much more rapid, and bordered
by rough banks, along which there is some scrambling to be done, and from the start to the finish

GUALEN LODGE.

of the Gualen water angling is downright hard
work. Although not large, the pools are numerous,
each requiring neat and precise casting, the best
perhaps being "Craggie" and the Stone Pool.
There is also a good cast on the stream between

Loch Dionard and the small loch above, from
which as many as seven fish have been had in
a day, a performance which in July, 1898, was
exactly equalled by Mr. Cecil Johnson, a friend of
Mr. Austen Leigh. In the old times, however,
Mr. Trevillian, the previous tenant of Gualen, often
had days of fourteen, twelve, ten, and eight fish;
now, however, there is but a very small chance of
such good sport, though why that should be so is
quite a puzzle, as for some years the bag nets have
been removed from Balnakill Bay, so that now the
Dionard has no nets working nearer to its mouth
than those of Loch Erribol on the east, while
the nearest on the west are those placed a little to
the north of Kinlochbervie on Loch Inchard, a
distance of fully forty miles.   Notwithstanding this
and the fact of there being fine spawning-grounds,
and neither obstructions, pollutions, or disease, the
angling is steadily deteriorating instead of improving.   Can poaching be the cause?—for the
steam trawlers, doubtlessly, poach many fish from

the Kyle. Is the damage they do—to which must be added the milder depredations of certain yachts and bands of natives — sufficient to account for the standstill of this river at its lowest point, when all the surroundings should lead to certain improvement ?

The Gualen rods, and they work hard, average about sixty salmon and grilse, and eighty sea trout a season—not a very brilliant return for the labour involved. Only a heavy rainfall brings the upper waters into order, and as it runs down very quickly, to ensure sport it must be got to at once. To reach it involves a rough and wet two hours tramp ere the rod can be put together; then the same journey has to be made at the end of the day, so it will be seen that angling on these upper Dionard reaches entails considerable hard work. A feature of the Kyle of Durness is the sea trout fishing in the salt water; at the half tides the currents run strongly, and in these the Durness Hotel visitors spin the natural sand eel with great sureness. On July the 4th, 1898, Mr. and Mrs. Trickett got in this way in one day forty sea trout weighing ninety-two-and-a-half pounds, and on the 28th of June another twenty-two weighing sixty-two pounds, the largest six-and-a-half pounds, the smallest one-and-a-half. Close to the hotel is also Loch Craspul, which at one period has evidently been connected with the sea, and in it there are fish which are doubtlessly land-locked sea trout, bright silvery fellows, very shy and tender in the mouth, and only to be deceived by the finest tackle and very small flies.

CHAPTER IX.

THE FLEET.

THIS small river, which drains seventy-three square
miles, opens on the 24th of February, and is netted
till the 10th of September (ten days more than it
should be), and fished by rod till the 31st of
October. Rising at an altitude of 750 feet above
sea-level, after a run of twelve miles it falls into
the Dornoch Firth, two miles to the south of
Golspie. The mouth is crossed by a viaduct just
a thousand yards long, over which passes the high
road from Golspie to Dornoch; in this there are
four arches with sluices, which keep in due
bounds the currents of the river and the tides, the
chief outlet being at the north end of the viaduct
and within a few yards of the Mound Station.

Above this viaduct the dammed back-waters form
a reedy, swampy lake, and further up the lower
part of the river is nearly all dead water, yielding
but little sport with salmon, though at times sea
trout are got.   Fish do not enter the river until
the first flood at the end of June or early in July,
and it is a curious fact that it should be such a
late river, sandwiched as it is between the Brora
and Helmsdale on the north and the Kyle of
Sutherland rivers on the south, all of which are
early ones.   This little stream, however, has one
peculiarity, without which it would hardly be worth
mentioning as a salmon river, for it is the only
place in Scotland where salmon are regularly killed
by rod and fly in salt water.   About three miles
seawards from the Fleet mouth is a stretch of salt
water called Loch Fleet, in which about an hour
after the tide ebbs a current is formed, which runs
with all the rapidity of a strong river stream, and
in this salmon are taken with rod and fly.

A further feature of the Fleet is the remarkable

salmon ladder at Torbol, on the Carnach, a tributary
on which there is a series of falls some sixty feet
in height, up which the fish have been successfully
taken.   The late Mr. Bateson, of Cambusmore—
which is at present rented by Mr. Laurence Hardy,
M.P.—was, I believe, the inventor and engineer of
this, the first fish-pass (about 1864) that took fish
up such a very formidable obstruction.

The total length of the pass, which cost £600,
is three hundred and seventy-eight yards, the first
one hundred and forty of which are very steep, up
which ascent the fish are taken by the ingenious
principle of a ladder within a ladder, which pro-
vides two sets of pools, a larger and a smaller, in
the breadth of the ladder, a large one on the right
hand side and a small one on the left.   In the
step below the order is reversed, and the fish is
thus enabled to pass alternately from shallow to
deep, and *vice versâ.*   At the head of the ladder a
sluice regulates the water flow, admitting only what
is required for the passage of the fish.   Salmon,

grilse, and sea trout ascended in fair numbers, and the waters above the fall soon became stocked and yielded sport to the rod.

The Cambusmore shooting on the south bank of the Fleet has the lower fishing of the river. Earl Amherst, at Morvich, on the north bank, and Mr. H. H. Bolton, at Rovie, have the remainder. The angler on the lower reaches of the Fleet is daily looked down on by the monument on Golspie Hill, erected to the memory of one of the late Dukes of Sutherland, the same duke who, at his own expense, emigrated so many of his crofters, greatly to their benefit ; and tradition relates that after the putting up of the monument some wag scribbled on its base the following lines—

> There was once a great Duke of Sutherland,
> Whose crofters were fond of their motherland ;
> But to each one he said, your passage is paid,
> And off you must go to some other land.

I vouch not for the truth of this story, but at any rate the lines are rather funny.

Chapter X.

THE FORSS, BY THURSO,

FLOWS out of Loch Shurrery, and after a run of twelve miles through the properties of Westfield and Forss, in which it drains fifty-eight square miles, falls into the North Sea six miles to the west of Thurso. There are good spawning-grounds above the Loch to which salmon, grilse, and sea trout ascend, and are there taken with the fly. From Westfield Bridge, five miles out of Thurso and just beyond the pretty little shooting lodge of the same name, down to the sea is about six miles.

At this bridge the Forss is narrow, shallow, and streamy, but as it flows through the green strath it opens out and forms plenty of pools, which about a mile above Forss Bridge become deep and still and require a good breeze for angling. Immediately below Forss Bridge come the falls of some thirty feet; but, as the illustration will show, they are so broken as to offer no serious bar to ascending fish, which make the passage from the left of the fall up the right centre.

From the Falls to the sea is about a mile—all dead water, which is good fishing on a day with a strong north wind blowing, though even should it be due south, so stagnant is this part that sport may yet be had by fishing the water up stream.

The river opens on the 11th of February with the usual close time for nets and rods, but inasmuch as the rivers close by both to the east and west open for the rod on the 11th of January, it seems only fair that the same privilege should be given to the Forss, and it would be better for the river if it were opened to the rod on the 11th of January and closed on the 15th of October, instead of the 31st, which would save the lives of a good few spawners. The netting time should

r ....ts an l r..ls, but inas-
... l y both to the east and
on the 11th of January, it
.. same privilege should be
i it would be better for the
... clos rol on the 11th of
... the 15th of October,
...ich would save the lives
... The netting time should

FALLS OF FORSS

be maintained as at present, or better still, be knocked off on the 15th of August instead of the 26th. March and April are the best months for spring salmon, and September and October for late fish ; the former average ten pounds, the latter seven pounds. Grilse run towards the end of July and average five pounds, while there are but very few sea trout.

Any of the standard flies of medium size will kill, but of course the smaller the water the smaller the fly. A light grilse rod will do all the work, and no waders are wanted.

The Forss fishing is let with Forss House and shootings, from the 1st of August, the spring fishing being let separately, and anglers can get comfortable quarters at a well-built modern farm-house just on the west of Forss Bridge and close to the river. Applications may be made to Mr. Alexander Mackay, at Forss House, of which he has a long lease. This house, so prettily placed by the Falls, has the advantage of being

well timbered, which, in the nearly treeless county
of Caithness, is a great attraction to all the small
birds of the neighbourhood, and the rookery is of
remarkable dimensions. This ancient house also
contains the two centuries old wooden stirrup-cup
of Forss; round it is carved, in curious letters and
odd spelling—

ATT everey Bout
Drink it Out;

but as it holds more than a pint, it is to be hoped
it was not filled with anything stronger than claret
or ale.

The Fishery Board Report for 1883 says that
in 1882 Macnicoll, the then keeper, had a day of
eleven fish, and altogether a total of forty-six in
six days; that in 1884 the take to the rod
was two hundred fish, which had been gradually
increased from fifty or sixty to that respectable
total by the aid of a hatchery started some seven
years earlier by Mr. Pilkington, and now removed
to Sandside. The 1883 Report also says that

Macnicoll marked many smolts, some of which were
got as salmon in the Duncansby head nets twenty-
five miles to the east of Forss mouth. It is to be
regretted the Report does not state the time that
lapsed between the marking of the smolts and their
being taken as *salmon*.

The fishing has gone off since the days of
Macnicoll, and perhaps the removal of the hatchery
has had something to do with it, for of late years
there is no record of any take approaching two
hundred fish. In 1892 two rods got one hundred
and sixty fish in March and April; in 1894 other
two had fifty; in 1898 Sir Redvers Buller and
Colonel Wyburgh had thirty from the 1st of March
to middle of April; and in 1899 John Black, the
present keeper, did not make up twenty for the
spring, which is only in accord with the poor sport
had nearly everywhere else this bad season.

In 1892 Colonel Philpotts had the water, and after
a blank fortnight he had two days of seven and five
fish, the start of these good times being commenced

with a false step and a header into deep water! but the gallant Colonel only laughed at his misfortune, quickly changed his clothes, and was then rewarded by the seven fish.

The mouth of the Forss is small, shallow and rocky. The bag-nets there are undoubtedly illegally fixed, and have been reported as such by Mr. Archer, but nothing has been done, except that the renter of the nets has offered Mr. Mackay an extra twelve hours weekly slap, a compromise which, though he has accepted it, is, nevertheless, a bad precedent, and does not do away with the fact that the tacksman is breaking the law, to which the attention of the authorities has been directed by the Head Inspector of the Fishery Board, and no notice taken.

In connection with the Forss there is also one of those anomalies which may occasionally be found in other rivers, for, though Sir Tollemach Sinclair owns the whole of the last mile and a half of the left bank, he has neither netting or angling right in the river.

CHAPTER XI.

THE HALLADALE.

SUPPOSED to take its name from a son of the first
Earl of Orkney, one Halladha, who was killed in
a battle in the Strath, and buried where he fell;
the field is still pointed out by the natives, a deep,
circular trench with a stone in the centre, marking
the burial-place of Halladha and his sword.

Draining an area of one hundred and eight
square miles, this river rises in the Knockfin
heights close to the Caithness border, and the same
slopes that send out the Berriedale from their south
sides discharge their waters as the Halladale on the
northern ones. The river is the boundary between
Caithness and Sutherland, and after a fairly rapid
run of twenty-two miles it falls into the North Sea

at Melvich Bay. There are no pollutions or obstructions, and the spawning-grounds are good. In order to reclaim some lands from the river, the grandfather of the present Duke of Sutherland cut the lower part of it into a canal, and though he gained his object, he spoilt this part of the river for angling, for it is now useless except with a strong breeze blowing up or down it, but up for choice. In those days the land was worth more than angling, nowadays the angling would be worth a great deal more than the land. Heather-clad hills are on both banks of the water, which is divided into six beats, the two upper ones of but little use, as the river runs down so very quickly; the four lower ones contain a number of pretty pools, which will give fair sport in continuously wet weather, especially after the nets come off.

At present the beats are divided as follows from the top: Forsinard Hotel has one rod; Forsinard Shooting, now rented by Mr. W. H. Fox, has two; Bighouse Shooting has one; Mr. Pilking-

ton, of Sandside, has one; and Melvich Hotel one.
They are fished in rotation, No. 6 being nearest
to the sea. During the spring the rods of Forsinard, Bighouse, and Sandside are often let, and
application should be made to the hotels at Forsi-

HAVICH POOL, HALLADALE.

nard or Melvich. As the top of beat No. 6 is fully
fifteen miles from Forsinard, and the bottom of
No. 1 is the same distance from Melvich, the angler
will do well to come to an agreement about the
cost of conveyance per week.

Each beat has a few good pools, the three best being " Foresel," " Havich," and " Ashel."

The best months for salmon are March and April, though the river opens to the rod on the 11th of January and closes on the 30th of September. The nets commence on the 11th of February and come off on the 26th of August. The Silver Doctor and Jock Scot, from medium to the smallest sizes, are the favourite flies. A grilse rod will do all the work easily; indeed, a trout rod will do it more comfortably. Knee boots or stockings may be wanted in the spring while the water is large, but as soon as it falls to a medium height no waders are necessary. The mouth is hard fished by half a dozen bag nets and a draft net and coble; and these fishings, at one time, were very remunerative, but have now fallen off, owing to the excessive slaughter of fish.

The Fishery Board Report of 1888 states that from the net fishings of the Strathy and Halladale, which cover some twenty miles of coast, the yield of the three previous years was an average of nine hundred salmon and four thousand grilse—rough on the grilse, and a certain method of diminishing the supply of salmon. During these three years, which gave two thousand seven hundred salmon and twelve thousand grilse, the rods took less than three hundred fish from the two streams!

The Halladale is another of the rivers for which Mr. Box, the Duke of Sutherland's factor at Tongue, has so long, but, alas! so ineffectually, advocated a shortening of the netting time by ten days, and making them cease to work on the 15th of August instead of on the 26th.

The average take of the river of late years is about sixty fish a season, rather under than over. In April there are a few sea trout to be got in the tidal water between Melvich Bridge and the sea ; but this is open to any one, and hard fished by the natives.

The Melvich Hotel is one of those trouting centres from which good loch fishing may be had

by the public, for it can have the run of some
thirty lochs, which are very wisely restocked each
season with Loch Leven trout from the Brora
Hatchery.

When I was at Melvich on the 6th of June,
the hotel was so full of trout fishers that there
was not a bedroom to be had in it, and I was
quartered out. It was the first of these hotels I
had stayed at, but I found all of them about
equally crowded. In Sutherland alone there are
ten of these trouting hotels, all of them fairly well
managed. They are those of Lairg, Forsinard,
Altnaharra, Tongue, Durness, Riconich, Scourie,
Altnacealgach, Inchnadampf, and Loch Inver.

The large sums spent by anglers for the
privilege of catching loch trout surprised me greatly.
At the lowest computation the hotel bill will come
to 15s. a day, the ghillie is 3s. 6d., with a further
1s. 9d. for his lunch; while more often than not
there is another 5s. a day as a share of a machine.
Here, then, we have numbers of fishermen paying

from 25*s.* to 30*s.* a day for the privilege of catching
from a dozen to four dozen loch trout, which, even
with "hotel weights," barely average three to the
pound, and in many cases very much less. The
take will, of course, depend on the combined skill
of the angler and his boatman, and the state of the
weather. Between these ten hotels there are
certainly seventy anglers spending 25*s.* a day each,
which is £612 10*s.* per week, and as the trouting
season lasts for some sixteen weeks, they disburse
in this County alone some £10,000 in pursuit of
their sport! Yet there is a yearly difficulty in
getting Parliament to make a close time for these
little fishes that bring such large sums into places
which would hardly be visited were it not for their
speckled attractions. This calculation is much
under the mark, for many of the trout fishers
are accompanied by their families, and spend a
great deal more on the hotel bill than my modest
estimate of 15*s.* a day, for I met several families
who must have daily spent ten times that amount.

On leaving Melvich I partly drove and partly walked up The Halladale to Forsinard, and was much struck with the numbers and well-to-do appearance of the crofters' houses, of which there must be several hundreds, and it speaks well for them |that cases of river poaching are few and far between. On my way I was interested by watching two families of peewits running about on a patch of short grass, the old birds looking on proudly until a "hoodie" appeared on the scene and made a dash for a breakfast at one of the young ones, a purpose which the united attack of the four old birds speedily defeated.

Forsinard Hotel is another of those trouting centres which are open to the public, worked very much on similar lines to Melvich. There are, perhaps, a few less available lochs, but the fish book and the stuffed trout in the hall bear witness that there is sport to be had. A ferox of ten pounds and a quarter taken from Badenloch by Mr. Priestley Edwards on the 20th of May, 1897,

brown trout of six pounds and three-quarters and
five pounds, and two others of four pounds, are
beauties to look at. From Loch Sletill, near Forsinard, on the Bighouse Shootings, a gentleman and
the keeper killed, some twenty years ago, one
hundred and twenty trout, which weighed eighty-
seven pounds. At Forsinard also the lochs are
restocked each year from the Brora Hatchery.

Chapter XII.

THE HELMSDALE, OR KILDONAN,

Is one of the best, if not the very best, of the early angling rivers, so much so that in the beginning of this century it is recorded that on the day before Christmas Day sixty clean salmon were taken from the Manse Pool at one haul of the net. Rising from several streams which drain the lochs lying around the foot of Ben Griam More, the two main ones unite near Kinbrace and form the Helm, which then flows for twenty miles, without obstructions or pollution, through Kildonan Strath, and falls into the sea at Helmsdale. Below Kinbrace it is joined by an important tributary which drains a chain of lochs of some 2,500 acres in extent, of which Loch-na-Moin is the lowest and is counted as a "beat" on the river; and during its course the Helm, which remains in good order for several days after a flood, offers the angler every variety of casting, and will test his skill to the utmost.

The angling goes with the six shooting lodges on the banks, and is entirely private and not let from the Sutherland estate office. At times, however, when some of the shooting tenants cannot get north for the spring fishing, they let their rods to friends. At the present moment these shootings are held as follows :—

Auchintoul Lodge, or the "Burn Field," on the left bank, is rented by Mr. F. G. Nutting; next, some ten miles below it on the same bank, comes Suisgill, or "Roaring Burn," a lodge originally built by Colonel Hunt, afterwards rented for some seasons by my old friend Colonel John Hargreaves, and now occupied by Mr. Leopold Hirsch. Five miles lower down and still on the same bank is Kildonan Lodge (Donan's Cell, an ancient Culdee

Saint), for many years in the possession of another old friend, the late Mr. Hamilton Bruce, and subsequently rented by Mr. T. Gardiner Muir, and at present vacant, owing to the sudden death of Mr. H. E. M. Davies.

While waiting on Kildonan Bridge this last June, I met Andrew Ross, the keeper there, and in the course of a chat with him, he asked me if I could suggest any explanation of a curious thing he had seen on the hill a few days before when watching a herd of deer. Not wishing to disturb them he had hidden, and while concealed, a hen grouse flew by, and settling near him, commenced to peck viciously at something. Anxious to see what it was, Ross rose suddenly and frightened her away, and on going to where she had risen from, there he found a newly-laid grouse egg partially destroyed. Ross was strongly of opinion the bird brought the egg in her claws, and did not lay it after settling, for she began to peck at the very moment she lit. Could this have been an old hen past breeding, that had taken an egg from the nest of a younger hen and was destroying it in a fit of jealousy ?

Now, to return to the Helmsdale Lodges. Six miles further on is Torrish, "the Fort by the water," held for upwards of thirty years by Mr. Alexander Macfarlan, and to his kindness I am indebted for my first cast on the Helm, as on the 8th of June of this year he magnanimously gave me his turn on No. 6 beat, which, as the river was dead low, offered, from its many rushing narrow streams, nearly the only chance of sport ; and from the Rock Pool I took the two smallest grilse I have ever caught—just two and a half pounds each ! So small did they seem to me that I would have it they were sea trout, and not until I compared one with the other was I fully convinced. When the two are laid side by side, it will be seen that the sea trout has a straighter tail than the grilse, also he has more spots, and on both sides of the lateral line, while on the lower side the grilse seldom has any spots : there may be at times one or two, but never many.

The other two lodges are on the right bank of the river, the more northern being Badenloch, rented by Messrs. F. and J. B. Taylor, and the other, some twenty miles from Helmsdale, Borrobol, may be said to have had but one tenant ever since it was first let, for Mr. F. Sykes, the present one, succeeded to his father, who was the first occupant.

These six lodges divide the whole water into twelve beats, six upper and six lower ones, each getting two beats a day, to one of which they can send a friend. Kildonan Bridge is at the top of the lower beats, and is No. 6, and the rod having No. 6 on the lower beat has also No. 6 on the upper beat, and so on all down the water. Beat No. 1 is nearest the sea, and Torrish always starts the season on it and sets the rotation for all the other five lodges.

The river opens for the rod on the 11th of
January, and closes on the 30th of September.
The nets begin work on the 11th of February,
and continue till the 26th of August; but I cannot
help thinking it would be better for the river, and
eventually show a greatly increased yield of fish, if
the nets ceased on the 15th of August and the
rods on the 15th of September

The best months for salmon are March and
April, and for grilse any time after the first spate
that comes at the end of May. Salmon average
ten pounds and grilse five pounds. In the early
part of the season an eighteen-foot rod and heavy
line, and wading trousers, will be required. In
April a rod of sixteen feet will do, and then, after
the middle of May, a stout trout rod is handiest;
and further on there will be found a graphic
account of what may be accomplished with so small
a wand of attack. Fly is the only lure used; sizes
ranging from 7/0 to 4/0 in the early months, and
gradually decreasing to the smallest double hooks.

With the exception of the Blue Doctor, all the standard patterns kill, although Walter Mackay, the Torrish keeper, prefers the Black Doctor dressed with a Guinea fowl hackle at the shoulder, in lieu of the usual one of claret. Mackay also swears by an invention of his own, "the Torrish Favourite," a pretty fly which he dresses as follows :—

Tag : Silver twist ; yellow floss-silk.

Tail : Gold pheasant topping ; black ostrich but.

Body : Yellow floss-silk half-way, the remainder yellow and red mohair ; silver tinsel all the way up ; ginger hackle tied in half-way ; guinea-fowl hackle at shoulder ; bronze turkey wing with gold pheasant topping over.

"Joe Brady" is also a good killer, the dressing being nearly the same as that of "The Torrish," already described in the chapter on the Brora. The beats are divided as under, starting from the sea up :—

BEAT No. 1.

(From the sea to Soliscraggy Bridge; best in
big water.)

Pool 1. Flat or Black Pool. In 1895 Captain
G. W. Hunt had ten fish one day from
this.

„ 2. Marrel. Good in big water.

„ 3. Lower Caen.

„ 4. Upper Caen.

„ 5. Railway Bridge.

„ 6. Sand.

„ 7. Jones'.

„ 8. Alder.

„ 9. Stall. Best fished from right bank.

„ 10. Soliscraggy. In 1895 Mr. Parker took
fifteen fish in one day here; also a
good grilse cast.

The whole of this beat fishes best in spring
with plenty of water. At Soliscraggy Bridge, on
the left bank, there is a pretty little cottage of the
same name which goes with the Badenloch beat,

while near it is Birchwood Cottage, which goes with Auchintoul, and from these two charming little houses the occupants of these respective beats carry on the spring angling.

BEAT No. 2.

(From Soliscraggy Bridge to Upper Torrish Park.)
Fishes best in spring.

Pool 1. Kilpheddar.

,,   2. Eldrable. Fishes well on both sides.

,,   3. Gate. Best on right bank.

,,   4. Park. Best from left bank.

,,   5. Carew's. Best from left bank.

,,   6. Woody.

BEAT No. 3.

(From Torrish Burn to the Big Tree on the left bank at the Big Bay.)

Pool 1. Lower Torrish ⎱ Two of the best on the

,,   2. Upper Torrish ⎰   river.

,,   3. Tail and part of the Bay.

A very fine beat in spring, from which ten to fifteen fish have often been had.

The late Mr. R. K. Dawson had fifteen one day, and Mr. Charles Ackroyd twelve.

BEAT No. 4.

(From lower end of Baddie Wood Pool to Killearnan Dyke.)

Pool 1. Baddan. Here in 1895 Mr. Macfarlan had fourteen fish in three hours.

" 2. Stoney Point.

" 3. Dalhalmy Bridge.

" 4. Kelt's Den.

" 5. Dalhalmy.

" 6. Black Hole.

" 7. Killearnan Dyke.

A very good beat during the latter part of March and first half of April. When the weather is cold fish do not ascend much above the top of this until early in March. In milder weather they pass up much earlier.

BEAT No. 5.

(From the Boat Pool to Kildonan Dyke.)

Pool 1. Killearnan Boat Pool. In 1895 eighteen
fish were landed here in a day by
Mr. Wood.

,,   2. Ewe's Neuk.

,,   3. Foam.

,,   4. Deible. From this Colonel Hargreaves
got seven one day, and Mr. Gardiner
Muir a like number on another day.

,,   5. Short.

,,   6. Whinney.

,,   7. Kildonan Dyke. A good beat in March
and April.

BEAT No. 6.

(From the Manse to Kildonan Bridge.)

Pool 1. The Manse. One of the best; and
on this pool the late Mr. Rutherford,
an old Helm angler, once saw six

rods each with a fish on; also from this and the two Rock Pools Mr. Ashworth landed sixteen fish one day, Mr. A. K. Dawson had a day of fourteen, and Mr. C. Ackroyd one of sixteen.

Pool 2. The Little Rock.

,, 3. The New Little Rock.

,, 4. The Big Rock.

,, 5. The Flat.

,, 6. The Fall.

,, 7. The Rock. Here the late Mr. H. E. M. Davies had a day of eight.

,, 8. The Bridge.

As soon as the fish reach this beat it becomes perhaps the pick of the lot, for, in addition to being an excellent grilse beat, it is also not quite so dependent on rain as some of the others, there being many rapid rocky runs in it from which fish may be taken even in quite low water.

Upper Beat No. 1.

(From Kildonan Bridge to end of Suisgill Parapet.
Above the bridge are a few fine streams.)

Pool 1. Rock.

„   2. Bathing.

„   3. Pool in the Wood.   The best on the beat.
Above the wood a few streams.

Upper Beat No. 2.

(From lower end of Suisgill Parapet to the Island
above the surface-man's house at Old Suisgill.)

Pool 1. Consists of five little pools opposite Suisgill House.

„   2. Several streams up to Suisgill Burn.

„   3. Opposite Old Suisgill Lodge.

„   4. Old Suisgill.

„   5. Small pools up to Island.   Mr. Radcliffe
had twelve fish one day off this beat.

UPPER BEAT No. 3.

Pool 1. Flats.

„   2. Dalvuie.

„   3. Borrobol Bridge.

„   4. Red Brae.

„   5. Dalcharn.

„   6. Lower Chancellor.

„   7. The Den.

„   8. Upper Chancellor.

„   9. Gravelly Stream.

„ 10. Kinbrace Park.

„ 11. Kinbrace Bridge.

A very good April beat, from which, in 1896, a gentleman staying at Ross' Hotel, in Helmsdale, got eighty-one fish in ten days.

UPPER BEAT No. 4.

(From Kinbrace Bridge to junction of Badenloch and Auchintoul rivers.)

Pool 1. The Washing Pool.   Nine fish one day by Mr. H. Ackroyd.

Pool 2.   Black Bank.

,,   3.   Burnfort.

,,   4.   Black.

,,   5.   Junction.

Upper Beat No. 5.

(From Junction of rivers to Loch-na-Moin ; a few
small bits up to Crockan.)

Pool 1.   Crockan.   A number of small pools and
streams on this beat.

,,   2.   Still Water Pool.   Twenty-two fish in one
day by Mr. Buckley!

Upper Beat No. 6.

(Loch Ach-na-Moin.   Seven fish in a day by
Mrs. Hick and Mr. Ashworth.)

From the foregoing list it will be seen that
each of the beats can boast of some extra good
days.   With regard to the last mentioned but one,
Mr. J. E. Buckley, one of the editors and authors

of a series of books called "The Vertebrate Fauna of Scotland," has kindly sent me the following modest details.

"On June 9th, 1896, my beat was No. 5 on the upper water. The morning was dull and rather cold, and apparently a good fishing day. I was staying at Mr. Trotter's farmhouse close to the beat, and so commenced fishing about half-past four. The river was somewhat low, and as the stream at the head of 'Crocken' was not more than fifteen or twenty yards in length, the extent was very limited, for that was the only place in which fish could be expected to lay hold. However, I tried the lower and dead part of the pool, and although I hooked two fish they both got off, so I gave up trying that part and confined my attention to the stream.

"At half-past eight I had landed five fish, and then went in to breakfast, and at a little past nine I was at the same pool again, and got one more fish, and then thinking this small bit of water had

been pretty well disturbed, I left it for the long
deep 'Still Water Pool,' just below Loch-na-Moin
at the top of the beat, fully intending to return in
an hour or so, but 'Diis aliter visum,' for until
late in the evening I never got there again to
pick up the things I had left on the bank in the
morning.

"As I reached 'Still Water' I saw a fish jump
high up in the pool, and he hooked at the second
cast. Having landed him, I missed out a good piece
of water and went down at once to what I knew
was the best part of the pool. Then followed an
experience that happens to few fishermen in their
lives. The salmon, which were jumping and splashing incessantly, took the fly like mad creatures and
with extraordinary boldness, and scarcely was a cast
made without a rise ; indeed, it was hardly worth
while troubling about a fish if he did not take at
the second cast over him, for the next cast below
would be nearly certain to put up another one.

"Having landed three fish, I had the misfortune

to break my rod—a twelve-foot single-handed trout
rod—a fish taking the fly just as it was leaving
the water. I landed him, however, and then had
to walk back to the house, rather more than two
miles, to get another rod. This time I brought
with me a ten-foot one, with extra joints in case of
fresh accidents; but fully an hour and a half were
lost on the two journeys, and a few minutes wasted
on getting a little refreshment.

"Having fitted up the rod, I set to work again
on the same pool, and by half-past seven I had a
total score of twenty-two fish. Even as it was I
am almost convinced I could have got more, but,
curiously enough, the last two fish were the heaviest
of the day—fifteen pounds each—and gave a great
deal of trouble to land, and I was also getting
rather tired. The fish also at the end of the day
were not quite so keen at taking hold, for I rose
several in succession without getting fast, and
the last one came three times before he was
hooked.

"Such are the main features of this extraordinary day, but I will add a few details which
may be of interest, and also explain why I did not
get even more fish. I was fishing, as I usually do
when possible, without a ghillie, and for this work
a small rod is more convenient to bring fish to the
gaff, for though the river is narrow here, yet there
are no sloping sandy or gravelly banks on which to
run a fish ashore, and the water runs as deep at
the bankside as it does in the middle of the stream;
therefore a small rod was more handy for bringing
the fish near to the gaff, and often when just on
the point of being gaffed, it would make a bolt
under the bank and have to be coaxed out again
with care, an operation which often took up a lot
of time. Although using ordinary trout gut, and
though on several occasions taken into unpleasant
patches of weeds, I never had a break, nor, except
in Crocken, as already mentioned, did I lose more
than one other fish. I cannot say with what fly I
took the six fish from Crocken, but the sixteen

from Still Water Pool were all got with a 'Brown Dog' with jungle cock shoulder feathers.*

"Catching so many was done rather in a spirit of emulation, as when I had landed some sixteen I remembered that the late Mr. Richard Rutherford, of Kildonan, had often told me he had once had twenty-one fish, mostly grilse, in a day, so seeing my chance I tried to break that record. What I might have taken had I been accompanied by a ghillie and used a grilse rod is purely a matter of conjecture. I think it is not over estimating to put it at forty or fifty, for I was 'fast' all the time I was fishing.

"The total weight of my take was two hundred and thirteen pounds, or nearly ten pounds each. I was quite alone all day, and fished but the two pools named; in the evening the farmer helped me up to the road with the fish and carted them home.

---

* For dressing see River Shin.

"In conclusion, I hope brother anglers will not consider the foregoing account is given in any spirit of boasting, but take it as a simple record of a very marvellous day, a kind of day which falls to the lot of very few fishermen of even much larger experience and greater skill than the writer pretends to.

"Yours very truly,

"(Signed)   T. E. BUCKLEY."

The Duke of Sutherland keeps the netting of the river mouth in his own hands, and does not allow his boats to begin work before the 1st of May. His Grace's coast nets (see Brora), some fifty in number, are let to Messrs. Sellar, of Aberdeen, report says, for the modest sum of £250 a year, a small amount divided amongst six, and it is to be regretted the Helmsdale anglers did not take them into their own hands. Of course, the rent Messrs. Sellar pay is the smallest part of their outlay. They would have to spend the best part of £1,500 in the necessary plant, in putting up the fifty bag nets already alluded to in the Brora chapter, and in addition they would have to pay the wages of about thirty men each week. So that in order to recoup themselves they must take a great lot of fish which would otherwise make their way into Brora and Helmsdale.*

The Fishery Board Report for 1897 states that the bag nets and river nets of the Brora and Helmsdale took nearly nine thousand five hundred salmon and grilse, while the six rods of the Helmsdale and the two of the Brora got with the fly under eight hundred, a remarkably disproportionate return, though not so great as in some cases!

The rents paid for angling are much heavier than those paid for netting, and having regard to this it seems a short-sighted policy to let down the splendid sport hitherto enjoyed. A letter of the late Colonel Hargreaves to me, dated Suisgill, the

---

* See " Netting " in Vol. II.

28th of May, 1893, tells that up to the 15th of the month about five hundred and twenty-five fish had been caught, "a miserable bad record for the river!"

"During January and February the river was frozen; then the weather turned very warm, and when the fish came they ran right through and took the Kildonan Falls on the 8th of March, fully a month earlier than usual."

"Disease, I am sorry to say, is rife. The total of the Suisgill rod to date is but one hundred and thirty-one fish."

In 1897 the six rods got four hundred and sixty-one fish.

In 1898, six hundred and seventeen fish.

In 1899, up to the 30th of May, only two hundred and fifty-eight! And the two best days were five fish a day!

So it is to be hoped that something may be done to improve the angling once more to the former standard of excellence.

CHAPTER XIII.

THE HOPE.

THIS river, which drains eighty-one square miles
of a most mountainous country, is formed by three
small streams rising in the old Reay Forest, not very
far from Gobernuisgach Lodge; these uniting form
the Hope, which thence flows through Strathmore
under the birch-clad slopes of Ben Hope for some
seven miles, when it expands into Loch Hope—
a lovely sheet of water about six miles long, and
varying from two hundred to twelve hundred
yards in width. On leaving the loch the river
has a further flow of rather less than two miles
to the sea, into which it falls on the east side of
Loch Erribol—"the little town on a sandy beach."
The angling of the river somewhat resembles

that of the Awe, and between the foot of the
loch and the sea it goes with Hope Lodge—prettily
perched on a high bank overlooking the loch and
the top part of the river, a somewhat inaccessible
dwelling easiest reached by a yacht, and, failing
that, only to be arrived at by a long posting
journey of some seventy miles from Lairg, *viâ*
Altnaharra, Tongue, and the Moin.

This river opens to the rod on the 11th of
January and closes on the 10th of September, the
netting season being from the 11th of February to
the 26th of August. These dates are taken from
the latest "Table of Annual Close Times," printed
by the Fishery Board Report. But Duncan Ross,
who has been keeper at Hope for several years,
maintains that the river remains open to the rod
till the 15th of October. Why the salmon rod
season of the Hope should commence on the
11th of January is a perfect mystery, for no clean
fish are got before the middle of June. The
Fishery Board Report of 1884 specially states "this

is a late river, and that with it the late rivers begin." A few pages further on the same Report announces that "the Dionard is the first of the late rivers." But both statements are erroneous, for, as a matter of fact, the Kinloch is absolutely the

HOPE LODGE.

furthest east of the late rivers; from Kinloch mouth to the east they are all early, to the west they are all late.

Mr. Archibald Young, a former Inspector of Salmon Fisheries, tried to account for this lateness and earliness by the relative temperatures of the river and the sea water. His theory was that rivers flowing into the German Ocean were early because that sea was a cold one, and that the higher temperature of the fresh water of the rivers tempted fish in search of warmer quarters to enter them early in the year ; *vice versâ*, the temperature of the Atlantic, warmed by the Gulf Stream (does it make itself felt as far east as the mouth of the Kinloch ?), being warmer than the water of the west coast rivers, therefore induced the salmon to stay longer in the sea. Mr. Young states that these west coast streams have short courses, with their fountain-heads at considerable altitudes, and in winter and spring, sometimes even in early summer, they are snow-clad, and then every partial melting brings down torrents of ice-cold water. But surely the amount of snow-water that pours down such rivers as Naver, Thurso, Helmsdale, Beauly, Spey, Dee, etc., must be quite as cold as any that comes down the west coast rivers, for much more snow falls on the

east coast hills than on any of the high grounds
of the west coast. The icy water of the north and
east coast rivers must also flow more voluminously
and continue to run cold for a longer period than
any of the shorter streams rushing down Laxford
Inver, Kirkaig, Shiel, or Awe.

Again, on coming to the Lowlands, where there
are no high hills and comparatively little snow that
lies for any length of time, we find rivers like
Doon, Luce, Cree, Dee, Nith, and Annan, all of
which are late rivers, but whose waters must surely
be of a higher temperature than those of any of
the named east and north coast rivers.

Thus, with so many contradictory facts to deal
with, I cannot think that either the late Mr. Young
or any one else has at present solved the question
as to why some rivers are early and some late.

The best months on the Hope are July and
August, and when the river is in full ply, an
eighteen-foot rod and wading trousers are required.
The best killers are Jock Scot and Silver Doctor,

dressed on sizes from 2 to 6 Limerick hooks.
Between the loch and the sea there are seven good
pools, the most noted being " The Stable " and
" The House Pool," and to fish the whole of them,
down and back again, is a fair day's work. For
this stretch the average take of salmon and grilse
is about forty-five ; in 1897 fifty-five were killed,
of which the heaviest was twenty-four pounds.
Although disease made its first appearance in 1894,
yet the rod take is incomprehensibly small, if it be
remembered that there are no bag nets to the east
within twenty miles of Hope Mouth, and none
within forty miles on the west, and probably poaching by steam trawlers has something to do with
this poor return ; and the fact that also the sea
trout fishing has been going steadily back for the
last four years also points to poaching in some
direction.

When there is a spate, fish take the worm
freely, although neither phantom or prawn is of
any use. The flies for sea trout should be on the

small size, not larger than No. 9, and any of the standard patterns will kill; mallard wing and orange body being the local favourite, together with the March Brown and the Zulu. Salmon are taken in the Loch with the fly, both by casting and trolling it; other lures are of no use. The largest sea trout got on the Loch was fourteen pounds, and the heaviest salmon twenty-two pounds. For five years the late Lord Rutherford Clark had Hope Lodge, and during this period his son, Mr. T. Rutherford Clark, averaged from Loch Hope just one thousand pounds of sea trout each season to his own rod, his best day's take being one of fifty-seven pounds.

Salmon pass right through the Loch and ascend the Strathmore River at the head, and there, when there is rain, two, three and four fish a day are sometimes got, while later on this upper water is the chief spawning ground, though fish use both the Loch and the river below it. There are few prettier fisheries in Scotland than those attached to

Hope Lodge if the sport could but be largely improved, and with the immunity from bag nets that the river enjoys I am quite certain that it only requires careful observation to ensure that desirable end.

With regard to the close time, Duncan Ross writes me as follows: "I have never known a clean fish caught on the Hope before the 12th of June. I am certain it is a late river. Until 1889 it closed on the 10th of September, and I spoke to the late Duke about it. Lord Rutherford Clark got permission to fish until the 15th of October in 1889, and certainly the river should not be closed earlier. I am not sure if the Fishery Board comes further in the county than the Shin, so that the Duke can make local laws as he pleases; at any rate, the Fishery Board has nothing to do with watching the river in this part of the county."

Hitherto my travelling in these northern regions had been done by posting from place to place at the usual rate of 1s. 3d. a mile, plus threepence

per mile more for the driver. Sometimes the jehu
was charged for in the hotel bill, sometimes he was
not, and before I became aware of this difference in
custom, on several occasions I paid the driver his
mileage twice over, greatly to his joy and much to
my astonishment at his very profuse thanks; it is
therefore just as well to ascertain before starting if
his fee has been included in the hire bill.

On the day I wished to quit Tongue, the dog-
carts had all gone to the various hill lochs with the
trout-fishers, so I had perforce to make my first
acquaintance with Her Majesty's mail cart, and in
it I started from Tongue for Erribol Ferry, *en
route* to Durness, a cheap and comfortable ride of
some twenty-six miles for six shillings, with a tip of
half-a-crown to the well-mannered driver. The same
journey in a dog-cart would have cost thirty-nine
shillings, so from this time forward I often tried the
same method of progression, sometimes successfully,
sometimes disastrously. A crowded mail cart on a
wet day is horrid, and whatever the weather, it is

still more horrid when it carries natives who have
taken too much whiskey, and who when started
produce bottles of it from their pockets and suck
at them until they are incapable!

For the benefit of those who have not tried

THE MOIN REFUGE HOUSE.

this mode of travelling, here is an illustration of
Her Majesty's mail pulled up at the Moin Refuge
House ; usually, however, these mails are on four
wheels, and much roomier than the little gig that
did duty on the present occasion.

The Hope river is crossed by a ferry-boat working on a chain, and that negotiated, a further drive of two miles brings the traveller to Heulim Ferry on Loch Erribol, which here is some two miles wide. Of course on this day the heavy boat was on the other side, and as it was a dead calm it was a case of patience while they rowed back. When at length the boat touched shore the luggage was quickly stowed away, and there seemed every prospect of a long pull across: as we started, however, there came a sound as of a gigantic boiling kettle, and a few seconds later half a gale was coming off the sides of Foinavon directly down the Loch. Up went our sail, and lucky now that our craft was stoutly built, for it took us five tacks and nearly two hours to reach the opposite shore, and though there was a trap from Durness Hotel waiting to take us the remaining seven miles of the road, it was long past midnight before we reached that comfortable quarter.

CHAPTER XIV.

THE INCHARD.

THIS little river, the most northern on the West Coast, drains but sixteen square miles, and has its source in a series of lochs mostly grouped round the foot of "the white hill" of Foinavon, while the stony heights of Ben Arkle look down on the others. These lochs discharge their waters over a fall, at present impassable to salmon, into Loch Garbet More, which again empties itself by a mere burn into Loch Garbet Beg, out of which flows the rapid little Inchard, to discharge itself, after a run of rather less than a mile, into the salt water of Loch Inchard. As an angling river it is nearly worthless, for it is so full of rocks, and the run is so rapid that, except just where it leaves the loch,

there is hardly a resting-place for a fish.   Salmon,
grilse, and sea trout take it with a rush, and
ascend with one run into Loch Garbet Beg with
the first flood that comes after the middle of June ;
and here good sport may often be had, for as

INCHARD RIVER.

many as sixty salmon and grilse have been taken
in one season by one rod staying at Riconich, a
comfortable inn prettily placed at the head of
Loch Inchard.   From the 1st of July the angling
of the loch is let from the hotel at the rate

of £20 a month, limited to two rods; and
for those who like loch fishing, I do not
know of any better sport to be had for the
money in Scotland. The Hotel Fish Book,
which is kept with care and entered up daily,
told me that in 1898, from the 14th of June
to the 17th of September, Loch Garbet Beg
yielded forty-one salmon and grilse, and just
over six hundred sea trout, averaging one and
a quarter pounds, the largest being six and a
quarter pounds. As to the best month, much
depends on when rain comes; but, with
the weather right, I would take from the
middle of July to the middle of August as
the cream of it.

In 1889 the then landlord of Riconich Inn
reported to the Fishery Board a general falling-off
of salmon and sea trout angling in the district,
which he unhesitatingly attributed to excessive bag-
net fishing, coupled with the fact that the observance of the weekly close time by these nets was

the exception and not the rule!! Loch Garbet Beg is a little over a mile in length and about a half in width. The fish pass up into Garbet More, but owing to its great depth they are not often caught there, and the chief take is in Loch Garbet

LOCH GARBET BEG, WITH BEN ARKLE IN THE DISTANCE.

Beg. In these two lochs the bulk of the productive spawning must be done, for though fish spawn in the river, the bottom is so rocky and devoid of gravel, and the current so strong, that it is doubtful if much or any of the spawn deposited

there ever comes to maturity. A fourteen-foot
rod will do all the work, and the standard patterns
both of salmon and sea trout flies kill. With a
good stiff breeze, size No. 2 Limerick hooks might
be used for salmon, and from that to the smallest,
according to wind and light. In addition to this
salmon and sea trout loch the hotel has the right
of fishing upwards of sixty brown trout lochs, for
which no charge is made; there is also good sea
fishing close by, and five miles up Loch Inchard
the natives catch a good many sea trout in salt
water by baiting with a herring liver. I did not
see this done myself, but Mr. Smith, the present
tenant of Riconich, told me that he had often
witnessed it.

Not far from Riconich, on the Scourie Road,
there is a fresh water loch emptying into the sea
by a short burn, and as it is the lowest of a series
of small communicating lochs, it would add to the
Riconich fishing if money was spent in making an
easy run for salmon and sea trout. Rough efforts

have already been tried, and proved successful to a
limited extent, as sea trout have been caught in
the lowest loch, but not in the numbers they might
be if the work of facilitating their ascent was
properly taken in hand.

CHAPTER XV.

THE INVER

FLOWS out of Loch Assynt, which is some ten miles long by one broad ; it drains sixty-eight square miles, and after a run of six, falls into the sea at Loch Inver.   Although not a very large river, during its course it offers the fisherman every sort of casting and many opportunities of testing his skill, as from " Garrarie," the first pool below Loch Assynt, right down to the mouth it is an angler's ideal river, and sad it is to see such fine water so very short of fish.   At present the upper beat of the river goes with Tumore Lodge and shootings, and the lower beat with Glencanisp Forest, now occupied by Lord Brownlow ; as, however, the shooting tenants rarely come north

before the 1st of August, it has been arranged
that up to that date the upper beat can be fished
by visitors staying at Inchnadamph Hotel, and the
lower one by those of the Culag Hotel at Loch
Inver; at this latter place the lower beat is again
divided into two, and a charge of twelve and sixpence a day is made for each beat as soon as the
first fish has been caught on the lower one, which
would be very cheap *if* there were fish to be got!

The season opens on the 11th of February and
closes on the 26th of August for nets, and the
31st of October for rods, which is fifteen days too
late. As far as the river is concerned, this opening
date, like that of many other rivers, is an absolute
farce, for it is but very seldom—I may say never
nowadays—that clean fish are got before the end of
May. The 1884 Report of the Fishery Board
does mention that in one previous May two rods
took thirty-nine fish in that month; but so greatly
has the angling fallen away of late years, that it is
rare for a single clean fish to be got by the 1st of

June. I fished the Inver on the 20th of June this
year, and one salmon and one grilse was then the
total take, although the river had been previously
well tried ; a take of thirty-nine fish now goes
nearer to the total for the whole season than to that
of any one month.   I suppose rivers are opened
on the 11th of February, so that the coast nets
near by may commence work; nevertheless the
opening of rivers on the 11th of February, in
which there is never a clean fish until well-nigh
four months later, does seem an absurdity! The
Dionard, the Kirkaig, Fleet, Kinloch, and Laxford
are other examples in the county of Sutherland.
As times are at present, salmon and grilse enter
the river together and come up with the first
flood at the end of June or beginning of July,
which, with August, is the best time.   A grilse
rod of fifteen or sixteen feet will cover all the
water, while fine tackle and small flies are
necessary, and a one-and-a-half Limerick hook
would be a *very* large fly, only to be used in

big water; Jock Scot, the Blue and Black
Doctors, Childers and Green Highlander, all kill,
while Lord Brownlow tells me that when the
water is very low, he occasionally gets a fish
with a sort of small red spinner with a plain
turkey wing. In 1857, when I first fished this
river, sport was very good, for from three to
six fish a day was quite a common matter.
Since those days the fish would appear to have
changed their tastes, for we never took more
than two sorts of flies with us. One dressed
as follows was the favourite :—

Tag: Silver twist yellow floss silk.

Tail: Gold pheasant topping and blue chatterer.

Body: Dark blue floss silk, claret hackle and
gold tinsel with wide spirals, jay at shoulder wing,
mallard and two strands of blue and yellow macaw.
Our other stand-by had exactly the same dressing,
only the body was yellow floss instead of blue.

In those days, with these two flies we did great
execution amongst the Inver fish, and we noticed

one very curious thing. One of us, in sending for a fresh stock of flies, forwarded as a pattern an old one, which, he did not notice, had lost the short chatterer's feather from the side of the topping in the tail, and the fresh ones were of course sent without this adornment, which we thought could make no difference ; but, strange to relate, we could kill no fish with this batch of flies ! It may have been fancy, but we put it down to the absence of the little blue feather in the tail.

When the water is large, stockings or even trousers may be wanted on the upper beat, but these are easily dispensed with in summer time by those who are in good health, for in the hot weather of July and August it is a pleasure to wade, and if not going deeper than six inches above the knee it seldom does any harm.

The fish push up to Loch Assynt as the water permits, and there they are caught both with fly and minnow. The river has no obstructions or pollutions, while the spawning grounds are large and

THE MINISTER'S POOL OF THE INVER

good ; in fact, everything is so much in favour of
the fish that the remarkable scarcity can only be
attributed to the bag-nets on the coast, which have
quite ruined the angling.   This set of nets has for
many years been rented by Mr. Speedie, of Perth.
They consist of seven stations, commencing at Oldshoremore to the north of Kinlochbervie, and coming
south to Clachtoll, not very far from Inver mouth.

Each station works a good many bag-nets.   I
could not find out exactly how many, but not less
than five each.   In 1890 their take was 1677
salmon, averaging twelve pounds each ; 8031 grilse
of nearly six pounds each, and 531 sea trout, all
of which would have come to the Inchard, Laxford, Inver, or Kirkaig ; in the same year the
united take to rod and line of these four rivers
was about two hundred fish ! !*

Of late years the average take of salmon
and grilse is a little over a hundred fish, about

---

* See Chapter on "Netting" in Vol. II.

equally divided between the tenants of the two shootings and the two hotels already mentioned, but verily I believe that the Duke of Sutherland could easily make the angling of this river yield him £1000 a year without losing his netting rental, or, at any rate, but a very small part of it!*

On the Lower Beat, commencing from the sea, there are seventeen casts and some bits as follows :—

Pool 1. The Bridge Pool. Looks very good, but
        is not of much account.

 ,,   2. The Carpenters. A good cast, and here,
        in 1857, the author killed his first fish.

 ,,   3. The Rocky Pool.

 ,,   4. Little Rock.

 ,,   5. Mill Pool. A fine big pot.

 ,,   6. Hog's Back.

 ,,   7. Ladder. So called from an iron ladder
        fixed at the tail, by which the perpen-

* See Vol. IV., Chapter on "Rivers Capable of Improvement."

dicular cliff can be ascended and a fish followed into Hog's Back—a fine bit of sport, requiring an active man to carry it through, and even then the odds are in favour of the fish.

Pool 8. Grave Pool. So called from some large flat stones on the bank resembling grave-stones. At the tail of this there is another iron ladder for the same purpose as the one described above.

„ 9. Pollan. This is Lord Brownlow's favourite, and very good.

„ 10. Pollachree.

„ 11. Scramble. A big, fine pool.

„ 12. Corner Pool. Not an easy matter to reach it dry-shod, as the illustration will show.

„ 13. Red Pool. From this pool, in 1897, Lord Brownlow's butler and gardener, getting leave for a cast, had the luck to take the two biggest fish of the season—thirty-one and twenty-six pounds.

Pool 14. Island Pool.   Long, good, and pretty
         fishing.

„   15. Dyke Pool.

HUGH MACKAY FISHING THE CAST ABOVE THE CORNER POOL
OF THE INVER.

Pool 16. Whirlpool. One of the best.

„   17. The Long Pool. Also good.

Above this the Upper Beat begins with the

Deer Pool. In this stretch the river frequently
opens out into small lakelets; the water is shal-
lower than on the lower one, and the best time is
from the middle of August to the end of September, the Minister's Pool, the Narrows, and the
Black Pool being the best casts. One of the
features of the Assynt district is the great extent
and number of trouting lochs which can be fished
by anglers staying at the hotels of Culag, Inchnadamph, and Altnacealgach; they all lie on the last
thirty miles of the high road from Lairg to Loch
Inver, and for those who are fond of loch fishing
each offers plenty of attraction. From Altnacealgach as many as 22,000 trout have been caught in
a season, averaging three to the pound, while the
other two hotels are not far behind this score. In
some of the lochs there are ferox also to be got.
The charge for ghillies is 3s. 6d. a day and 1s. 9d.
for their lunch, which is rather too high for the
food. However, the season is short, and it is a
case of making hay while the sun shines.

I was much amused by the ghillie of a trout fisher who could not settle whether he would fish salt or fresh water. While his master went off to think matters over, Donald, with both hands thrust deep in his pockets, did his best to hold up the wall of the hotel. When his employer at last returned to say he would try the sea, Donald stolidly jerked himself upright and replied : " Well, sir, then I will just go west and get a bit piece." The kitchen was " west," and " the bit piece " half a loaf, with about a pound· of roast beef and two glasses of whiskey.

Chapter XVI.

THE KINLOCH

Drains seventy-three square miles of a very mountainous but grand country. Rising on the western slopes of rugged Ben Loyal, it flows out of Loch Derry, and has a short, tumbling run of three miles of pots and streams into the Kyle of Tongue. It rises and falls so rapidly that only those living on the banks can fish it with advantage. It is strictly private, the respective tenants of Kinloch Forest and Loch Loyal shootings having each a side of the water, which forms the march between the two places. It is a very late river, up which fish seldom come before the end of June or beginning of July; nevertheless, it opens to rod and net on the 11th of February; closes for nets on the

26th of August, while the rod can work on till the 31st of October. It can easily be covered with a light rod, and all the standard flies kill, but they must be small, and dressed on irons ranging from No. 2 to No. 6 Limerick hooks. No waders required. There are not many sea trout, or brown ones either. A friend of Mr. Lawson's, the late tenant of Kinloch, who now rents Loch Loyal shootings, had a day of five fish a few years back, quite a brilliant exception, for this is one of the most disappointing little streams in the north. From the end of July it swarms with fish, which (average nine pounds) rarely take any lure, although every sort has been tried.

Mr. A. Balfour is the present tenant of Kinloch Forest Lodge—very prettily placed on the heather high up over the river. In addition to this fishing there is also the right of a boat on Loch Hope, some eight miles across the hill by a pony-track. Salmon now ascend to Loch Derry with ease, though up till about fifteen years ago they could

not do so, when the late Duke of Sutherland put a
dam at the tail of the pool below the fall, and so raised
the water to such a height as would let the fish up.

KINLOCH RIVER AND LODGE.

I stayed at Tongue Hotel to explore this river,
and in the smoking room there I made the
acquaintance of Mr. Speedie, the renter of all the
Sutherland bag-nets of the west coast of the county.

Naturally I tried to get him to talk salmon, and opened up the conversation by an allusion to the very bad season of this year. Mr. Speedie did not seem in the least depressed by it, for he said he remembered seasons nearly, if not quite, as bad, which had in due course been followed by very good ones, and he confidently predicted a return of prosperity. Mr. Speedie likewise holds the opinion that in some rivers there are too many fish for the extent of the spawning ground, and that where such is the case they destroy each other's beds ; also that in other rivers there may be too many kelts, and in that case they eat nearly all the par.

I hope Mr. Speedie is right in being sanguine of a return of good times. Certainly there is the recorded fact in his favour that in the three years of 1850, 1851, and 1852, but an average of twelve thousand eight hundred and fifty-nine boxes of Scotch salmon were sent to Billingsgate, whereas in 1862, 1863, and 1864, this average was rather more than doubled !

One of the features of Tongue is the sea trout fishing in the Kyle by spinning a sand eel, where some very good takes have been occasionally made.

On the 1st of June, 1891, the Bishop of Sodor and Man had thirteen sea trout, weighing fifty-seven pounds, or over four pounds each. On the 15th of June, the day I was there this year, but one sea trout of three pounds, and thirty pounds of loch trout, were brought into the hotel, these latter being some of the pinkest and best-flavoured I ever ate. This, however, was a period of drought, which probably had something to do with the smallness of the take.

CHAPTER XVII.

THE KIRKAIG

DRAINS eighty square miles of country, and flows
from a series of lochs in Assynt, the chief of which
are Boarlan, Urigill, Cama, Veyatie and Fewin, this
latter being the nearest one to the sea. The river
also forms the boundary between the counties of
Ross and Sutherland, and about two and a half
miles from the sea the whole water is precipitated
down a perpendicular fall of some sixty feet in
height—a grand sight when the water is big. Up
this, of course, salmon cannot pass, and it is
between this and the sea that all sport is had,
including the deep, black, and somewhat uncanny-
looking pool at the foot of the fall.

There are twenty-three named casts in this

short stretch of water, and if fish were only more
plentiful, grand would be the sport offered by this
river, with its rapid streams, boiling pots, and rugged

FALLS OF KIRKAIG.

banks; for I know of no other river in Scotland
which requires such hard walking, so much
scrambling and careful placing of feet, as this
one. In many places the angler will have to

descend and then again ascend very steep rocky
banks for fully a hundred yards or more, and
repeat the same process to fish the next pool,
and as none of them are long or require much
time to cast, the amount of hard work for the
legs is out of all proportion to that called for from
the arms.

Like its neighbour, the Inver, this also is a very
late river, and of but little use before July, that
month with August being the best time. More
fish are taken, perhaps, in September, but by then
they are turning black. This river is also absurdly
opened on the 11th of February, closing for rods
on the 31st of October, and for nets on the
26th of August, both dates being quite fifteen days
too late.

A grilse rod and medium-sized standard flies
will do all the work, and no waders are wanted ;
the fly is usually the only lure used, but at times
a few fish have been got with a prawn.

. There are no nets at the mouth, and no

bag-nets nearer than Clachtoll to the north of
Inver mouth, and yet these bag-nets and those
working at Stoer Point further north appear to
sweep the sea of the fish that should come to the
Inver.

The Kirkaig salmon average eleven pounds,
and grilse fully five, and there are hardly any sea
trout. The usual take of recent years to the rod
is from forty to fifty fish, and in 1898 Mr. Lang-
more had the river for July and August, and was
thought very fortunate to get fifty-three salmon and
grilse in that period; but this gentleman, in addition
to being a good fisherman, was also a very hard
worker.

At present the angling is let to Mr. Mackenzie,
the landlord of the Culag Hotel at Loch Inver.
He divides it into two beats, on which there is
ample room, and charges 12s. 6d. a day to each
rod. The angling is all done from the right bank,
consequently it is a left-handed river; there is
hardly any spawning ground, and it is wonderful

how fish spawn in it at all. From the sea up the
Fall the pools run as follows :—

No. 1.   The Rock Pool.   Not of much good.

  „   2.   The Elders.   Good and large.

  „   3.   The Old Bridge Pool.   A very pretty and
             likely one.

  „   4.   Heather Pool.

  „   5.   Island Stream.   A big water catch.

  „   6.   Hazel.   Very good in high water.

  „   7.   Little Kirkaig.

  „   8.   Turn Pool.

  „   9.   Wether Pool.

  „   10. Red Pool, and two streams below.

Here the Lower Beat ends, and without any
time passed in "playing or landing" it will take
three hours' hard work to fish it up.

The Upper Beat is rather more "scrambly"
than the lower one.

No. 1.   The Shady Pool can only be reached by a
             very steep descent and a hard climb up
             again—is often passed on this account.

THE ARROW POOL OF THE KIRKAIG

No. 2. The Arrow Pool. Very good.

„ 3. The Bow.

„ 4. The Otter Pool. A fine one, which my ghillie would call the Orrter Pool.

„ 5. The Red Lamp Stream.

„ 6. Little Fall. A very big pot.

„ 7. Spring Pool. Good.

„ 8. Lower Nettle.

„ 9. Upper Nettle.

„ 10. Lower Smash.

„ 11. Upper Smash.

„ 12. The Fall Pool.

All these last three pools are separated from each other by wall-like cliffs descending sheer into deep water. The angler has to scramble up and down to fish each one, and as the names tell, it is quite impossible to follow a fish out of the two lower. It is just possible to follow out of the Fall Pool by coming up the bank, but the proceeding is very unlikely to end with flying colours.

The approach to this last-named pool was, until lately, a really nasty one, requiring quite a gymnastic performance. After a few times one got used to it, but the first attempt always puzzled a stranger—so much so, that a friend of mine slipped, fell, and bounded from the hard rock with a thud into the horrible black boiling pool below. Luckily he was not stunned or crippled, and being an extra good swimmer, with a very steady nerve, he came out none the worse; but had he not possessed these qualifications his chance would indeed have been a poor one. The approach has now been made easier, and is nothing to be dreaded.

When there are fish in the river they may be seen continually jumping at the fall: a hopeless task, but a matter that the fish seem very slow to learn. The Kirkaig fish used to be considerably larger than those of the Inver, for when I was fishing the latter river in 1857 the gentleman who had the Kirkaig also lived at Loch Inver Hotel;

I think it was Sir Wroth Lethbridge, but, whoever it was, I recollect he was daily bringing in
three or four fish, amongst which would be at
least one of fifteen to twenty pounds; indeed, they
have been caught of much heavier weight, even
up to thirty-eight pounds, though not of recent
years. The late Duke of Sutherland and also the
present Duke have at various times considered the
question of taking the salmon round these Kirkaig
Falls, but up to the present the expense of
opening them has been considered too large for
the prospective benefits to be gained. There is
one thing, however, to be said, viz., that these
falls and the whole of the chain of Kirkaig lochs
are entirely on the Duke's ground, so that if they
were opened up there would not be any fear of
such litigation as is threatened by the much easier
opening up of the Falls of Mounessie on the
Spean, for there the country to be salmonised,
that lies above the falls, belongs to the representatives of the late Colonel Walker, of Inverlair, and

above him to the Mackintosh; both properties
being in the Lochaber district, over which Lord
Abinger claims the whole of the salmon fishing
rights.

From the top of the fall the river up to Loch
Fewin has many fine pools; the loch itself is a
narrow one of considerable length and covers
three hundred and seven acres ; above this the
river runs for nearly a mile over some fine spawning ground, and then comes Loch Veyatie, four
miles long, with an area of nearly six hundred
acres.   A short, big stream connects this with
Loch Cama, a sheet of water of about the same
size, and close to the Loch are the Black Falls,
of considerable height, so that unless these falls
were opened up also it would not be of much
use opening up those of the Kirkaig alone.
With both falls clear for salmon, Lochs Fewin,
Veyatie, Cama, and Boarlan, and all the streams
connecting them would be salmonised — that is,
seven miles of river and one thousand eight

hundred acres of lochs.* The question is, would it pay?—and until that can be answered in the affirmative, I think the Duke is quite right to leave matters as they are, for he owns other rivers on which he could experiment at a less cost, and unless one has seen the Kirkaig falls and walked the loch country beyond, it is impossible to form any idea of the magnitude and cost of making this experiment.

* See "Obstructions," Vol. II.

Chapter XVIII.

THE LAXFORD

DRAINS sixty-seven square miles of very rocky steep country, and has its source in several burns running into the head of Loch More, up which salmon used to find their way in the spawning season, but now, owing to the scarcity, they are seldom seen. Loch More is some three miles long, and about a half wide. At the west end it joins on to Little Loch More just opposite the Forest Lodge, rented for many years past by the Duke of Westminster. On issuing from this small loch, the river flows for about a mile through reedy, marshy ground, until it reaches Loch Stack, alongside of which, for about two miles and a half, is the high road to Scourie and Riconich. At Stack Lodge the river leaves the loch and has a run of about three miles into the sea at Loch Laxford. It is an angler's ideal river, with rapids and deep pools following each other in quick succession. For those who like hard work it is perhaps fished somewhat too easily, for no waders are wanted, while a good broad and well-kept path runs along each bank, the left one being the favourite.

The Duke of Westminster has the whole river, which is carefully preserved and opens at the odd date of the 11th of February. I say "odd" because it puzzles me to understand why a river should be declared "open" at that date when it is a well-known fact that before the 1st of June a clean-run fish is hardly ever seen in it, and even the bag-nets of this coast do not begin work until the end of March. Is this date thus fixed so early in the year still continued in memory of the old times, when angling for kelts, kelt-spearing, etc., was a common form of sport and amusement?

The right of fishing by net and coble at the

mouth is held by the Duke of Westminster, but is
not exercised, and though a watcher is kept there
to prevent poaching, yet the crews of lawless
steam trawlers often rob the Loch of quantities
of salmon and sea trout waiting for a rainfall
to take them up the river. Like many another
one, this renowned water has fallen on evil
times, for the angling has steadily and greatly
deteriorated during the last twenty years. The
Duke of Westminster usually gives the fishing for
July and August to Lord Leicester, and when he
first fished Laxford it was not an uncommon matter
for him to have eight or ten fish a day to his rod,
while one of his sons coming behind him would
have another four or five ; in these days the take
for the season used to be from two to three hundred
fish, and now it averages from fifty to sixty ! !

Adam Macaulay, the stalker at Stack Lodge,
has known the river for twenty-five years, and is
acquainted with every stone, and tells me that
there are not nearly one quarter of the fish on the

LUXFORD RIVER AND STACK LODGE

spawning beds now that there used to be twenty years ago, when he was accustomed to see fully a hundred pairs in about the three hundred yards of beds below Stack Bridge, while from ten to twelve couple were the most he could count last year!

"The capricious Laxford," as the Duke of Westminster calls it, although fed by two large lochs, yet rises and falls very quickly, for the surrounding hills are steep and the rain pours off them at once. Its salmon average eleven pounds, the grilse five and a half, and the sea trout one pound. It is but of little use fishing it before the 20th of June, unless there has been a spate just before that date. I fished it on the 17th of that month with Adam Macaulay as guide, and a pleasanter one could not be wished for; the river was then low, and beyond rising one fish twice I saw no sign of salmon, and Lord Zetland had had a try a few days previously with no better success.

July and August are the best months, and then salmon, grilse and sea trout all come together. Fine tackle, a sixteen-foot rod, and small flies of the standard patterns will do all that is necessary. It is seldom that any other lure is used, although one season, when Lord Cairns had Stack Lodge, he caught a few with the prawn; but by the middle of September the fish are turning colour, and certainly rod fishing should end on the 15th of October, if not on the 30th of September.

There are twenty-one good pools from Stack Lodge to the sea, and commencing with that immediately below the Loch, they come as follows :—

No. 1. Top Pool. A fine pool and one of the best ; fished from a jetty. The Hon. E. Coke had five here one day.

„ 2. Stream Pool.

„ 3. Mrs. Coke's Pool. Fishes best in big water.

„ 4. The Corner Pool.

No. 5. The Boat Pool. Here Lord Leicester
　　　had a very big fish on for four hours,
　　　which broke off without ever being
　　　seen.

　,, 6. Lord Anson's; or, The Island Pool. A
　　　deep still one.

　,, 7. The Duke's Pool. The best on the
　　　river; the head of it is a strong rush
　　　through a rocky gorge which will fish
　　　even in very low water; below, it
　　　opens out into a splendid pool of some
　　　length. As many as fourteen fish in
　　　the day have been taken here, but not
　　　of late years.

　,, 8. The Duchess Pool. Also a sure cast,
　　　and fished from a jetty of half-circle
　　　shape.

　,, 9. The Rock.

　,, 10. Lord Belgrave's. A high water catch.

　,, 11. Fern Pool. A long one.

　,, 12. John Macleod's. A rocky run.

No. 13. Mr. Leache's Pool. Out of this Lord
Henry Grosvenor took eighty sea trout
one day.

,, 14. Claughton's Pool.

,, 15. Brae Pool. A good long one ; here
Lady Mabel Coke rose ten fish, which
mostly came short, but four were
landed.

,, 16. Lord Dudley's Pool. He had the fishing
before the present tenants. Below this
are the old cruives.

,, 17. The Shepherd's Pool.

,, 18. The Bridge Pool.

When Lord Cairns had Stack Lodge, he, on
one occasion, arrived fishless at Laxford Bridge,
after having flogged the whole water down. On
looking over, he saw five fish lying near the
surface, but not very close to each other, and
happening to have a rifle with him, which he
had given his ghillie to carry on the chance of a
shot, he fired at the largest fish, which sank

mortally wounded, and drifting to the tail of the pool was pulled ashore. On again looking over the bridge, he noticed three others of these fish all kicking and gasping in a state of semi-consciousness, evidently produced by the concussion

LAXFORD BRIDGE.

caused by the discharge, or by the bullet striking the water, though it seemed impossible that from such a height such a small bullet, fired with a small charge of powder, could have produced this result, yet there were the fish; and as, just then,

the Duke of Westminster's yacht appeared steam-
ing up Laxford Loch, Lord Cairns, thinking His
Grace would like a fish for dinner, gaffed one
of them and gave it him as he passed. The other
two fish shortly recovered and swam about quite
right again.

There is no one with such an experience of
the salmon fishings of these parts as Mr. McIver,
of Scourie. Since 1845 he has managed for the
Duke of Sutherland, and he told me that when he
first took office the whole of the ducal nets were
then let to Messrs. Hogarth, of Aberdeen. There
were no estuary laws in those days, and the firm
fished very hard, both by bag nets in the sea,
which doubtlessly knew no weekly close time, and
by day and night with double sets of cobles and
nets at the mouth of the rivers. The first year
an enormous number of fish were taken, and the
profits were large ; the second season was fair,
though not so good as the first ; the third was
poor, and resulted in a loss ; the fourth gave

hardly a fish, and Messrs. Hogarth asked, as a favour, that they might be relieved of their lease. This shows very forcibly how quickly merciless netting, uncontrolled by law, can well-nigh exterminate salmon.

In this instance the havoc wrought by over-netting quickly came to a head, and vigorous measures eventually put matters right again ; but I am confident that a precisely similar disaster is slowly but surely overtaking the whole of our salmon fisheries. Unless the yearly and weekly close times are lengthened, unless the numbers of the bag nets are limited, and unless they are forced to observe the close times, this must be the inevitable result.

At the end of Hogarth's fourth year the nets were not fished for several seasons, with the result that the salmon quickly recovered from the ravages of the preceding years.

In 1890 Mr. McIver replied as follows to a question put to him by the Fishery Board :—

" The only suggestion that occurs to me, with

regard to this coast and the various rivers, is the subject of bag nets and their effect on the rivers.

" The angling is certainly not so productive as it was. Anglers invariably attribute this to the quantity caught in the bag nets. This may be partially correct, but when there is water in the rivers to enable the salmon to ascend, anglers have fair sport, and in some seasons, from natural causes, the numbers of fish are much smaller than in other seasons. The extension of the close time might meet this complaint on the part of anglers. There must necessarily be some means adopted to reduce the natural yearly increase of fish. A large number escape the bag nets placed now outside the estuaries, and in some cases miles away from the mouths of the rivers ; for when there is not sufficient water in the rivers to allow them to ascend, they are seen in numbers jumping in the sea at their mouths. But the rivers are short, and fall rapidly, and it is often the case that they are unable to get up for want of sufficient water.

"The netting, or setting of bag nets, might cease
earlier than the 26th of August, and might properly

.E. McIVER, Esq.

and beneficially be given up on the 1st of August
to allow fish to ascend the rivers after that date."

In 1885, 1886, and 1887, the bag nets of this
district took, between Oldshoremore Station on the
North and that of Clachtoll on the South, two
thousand six hundred and thirty-two salmon and
twenty-one thousand one hundred and fifteen grilse,
or more than eight babes to each adult. A large
proportion of these grilse are taken between the
1st and 26th of August, and if Mr. McIver's wise
suggestion were adopted the nets would soon be
killing as many salmon as grilse, while the angling
would become very much better, and consequently
very much more valuable than at present.

In reply to further questions Mr. McIver says :
" The bye-laws with regard to the annual close time
are fairly well kept, and surprise visits are made
every now and again to see that the bag-net leaders
are removed in terms of the bye-law."

To differ with such an eminent authority requires
some courage, but on Sundays I have visited several
netting stations on this coast, and can state that it
is *quite the exception to find the leads removed from*

the bag-nets, for, as a rule, the bulk of the "out-of-the-way ones" observe no weekly close time at all during the whole of the season. As to "surprise visits," very often the surpriser is father, brother, uncle, or cousin, and certainly friend, of the men who are to be surprised; therefore it is not to be wondered at that the bag-net people somehow or other get to know of the "surprise" before it takes place. I regard this fishing of bag-nets without any weekly close time as doing the very greatest harm to the angling of this district; it is nearly as bad as putting a net across the mouth of a river and never removing it.*

---

* See chapter on "Netting—Legal and Illegal," in Vol. II.

Chapter XIX.

THE NAVER

Drains one hundred and eighty-six square miles, and is the largest of the Sutherland rivers. It rises in several lochs draining into the Mudale and Vagastie streams which flow into Loch Naver, out of which the river runs. Of these two tributaries the Mudale is the largest, and rising in the northern slopes of Ben Hee, it drains Loch Meadie and then has a run of some dozen miles before it loses itself in Loch Naver at the foot of Ben Clibreck. This loch is about six miles long, with an average width of half a mile. It is a very early one, with the best angling at the upper end, where as many as six spring fish have been taken in a day, while a few years ago one rod had fifty-two in

seven weeks, mostly by trolling a phantom, though
they have been known to rise to a fly. There
are three boats on this loch : the hotel at
Altnaharra has one, Mr. Baxendale has another
with the Ben Clibreck shootings, and the third
goes with Syre Lodge.

Late in the season fish ascend the Mudale to
spawn and are occasionally caught, but as they are
then getting black, it is but seldom the rod is
plied on this tributary.

As the Naver leaves the loch it is joined by
the Mallart or Mallard, another considerable tributary flowing out of Loch Choire or Corr, and from
this point it has a run of some ten miles through
a barren-looking country until it reaches Syre, when
the banks become birch-clad, and after a further run
of twelve miles it falls into the sea at the sandy
bay of Torrisdale, about a mile below Bettyhill.

The rod season begins on the 11th of January and lasts till the 30th of September ; the
nets commence on the 26th of February, and

come off on the 26th of August, quite ten days too late.

The best months for salmon, which average thirteen pounds, are February and the two following ones, the very pick of it being from middle of March to middle of April. The grilse, average seven pounds, begin to run as early as May and continue for the following three months.

The use of a landing net is not compulsory. In early spring an eighteen-foot rod and wading trousers will be wanted, which, as the season advances, can be exchanged for a smaller rod and wading stockings. No other lure than the fly is allowed, and in addition to all the standard patterns, the Yellow and Grey Eagle of the Dee is also a killer. In the early spring, lures may be dressed on irons ranging from 7/o Limerick down to 1½, and then from the end of April they fall to the very smallest sizes.

This twenty-two miles of river is divided into six beats. Two rods go with the Syre shootings, which were for the past eleven years in the hands of the late Mr. G. D. Stibbard, and are now held by Mr. Dankwerts ; other two go with the Skelpick shootings, and the remaining two belong to Dalvina, a lodge nearly opposite Syre, until the

DALVINA LODGE, RIVER NAVER.

1st of August, when one of them goes to the tenant of Ben Clibreck shootings, at present occupied by Mr. Baxendale, the other remaining with Dalvina, but up till the 1st of August Mr. A. Brocklehurst has both rods.

At these three lodges anglers put up for the

spring; the shooting tenants themselves usually being the anglers. Sometimes it happens that there is a sublet, and anyone wishing to get a chance on the Naver cannot do better than communicate with Mr. Box at Tongue, who generally can say if there is likely to be a rod or two in the market. Whoever fishes No. 1, the top beat, on Monday, finishes on No. 6, the lowest, on Saturday, which order lasts all through the season. The rod on No. 1 Beat will then commence on No. 2 Beat in the next season, and so removes down a beat every year; a very slow process, and it would be merrier for all if Sunday were counted as a fishing day, by which arrangement the man who had started on No. 1 on Monday and fished No. 6 on Saturday would, in imagination, fish No. 1 again on Sunday, and go to No. 2 on Monday.

Skelpick Lodge, in addition to its rights over the different beats, has also a separate and exclusive one of its own, extending downwards for some two miles of both banks, and commencing from under the Lodge. The tenant, Mr. Erle Drax, who has fished the Naver off and on for the past thirty years, tells me the six rod holders pay

SKELPICK LODGE, RIVER NAVER.

£600 a year for the angling, but to secure sport they are obliged to rent the netting, so as to give a chance for the fish to enter the river, and consequently the net and coble at the mouth is

THE LOOK OUT AT NAVER MOUTH

not fished till the 1st of May, and even then it is not worked on Wednesdays.

In June last I stayed at Bettyhill Hotel to visit the Naver, and on the evening of my arrival I joined the "look-out" party on the high cliff overhanging Naver mouth, and saw them net a few grilse. It so happened that evening I was attacked by a fit of sleeplessness, so a little after midnight, in search of a soporific, I stole downstairs to the coffee-room, where I had noticed a few books; snatching them up, I retreated to my couch and commenced to examine them. The first had the not very cheerful title of "Early Graves," and was quickly discarded; the second selection was called "Elijah and Ahab;" while the inscription on the back of the third was "A Candle Lighted by the Lord," and the three combined titles had the desired effect without a perusal of the contents.

Each beat of the Naver has from nine to thirteen good pools.

THE LOOK OUT AT NAVER MOUTH

No. 1 is from " Dalmallard " to " Dalharrold."

Beat 2. From Syre Pool to Upper Craggie.

„ 3. From the Boat Pool to Dawson's Pool.

„ 4. From Ravigill to Achalmie.

„ 5. From Upper Carnasby to Dunvedin.

„ 6. From Dunvedin to Naver Bridge.

At the head of No. 1, near where the river leaves the loch, there are the falls of the Mallart, which have been laddered in recent years, so that the fish can pass up at any time. Before this was carried out they could only ascend at a certain height of water, which eventually came and took the fish up the falls to the spawning-grounds. It is the opinion of some of the Naver anglers that this ladder has to a great extent spoilt this No. 1 Beat, for before the days of the ladder, when fish became numerous in the Fall Pool, as soon as they found they could not pass up they fell back into the top pools of the beat, where they gave good sport. Some are also of opinion that a dam above the Creich Pool, a little distance below the loch, would

much improve the top beats, by forcing the fish
that could not pass over it with a medium water to
fall back and stock the pools below until a flood
came sufficiently heavy to take them up. A dam
of this sort was once made a little below the exit
from the loch, and though personally I do not think
that fish once arrived there would ever drop back
to stock the pools much below, as expected, the
question, as far as that particular dam was concerned, never had any chance of being settled, as
the first flood washed it away.

With regard to this, I have frequently seen
numbers of fish arrive in a fall pool to wait for
water to take them up, and there they stayed,
massed together, and, without dropping back to
pools below, there they stood out the drought, and
waited patiently till the rainfall came.

It is certainly a very curious thing that the
Naver take each season does not grow better and
better instead of falling off; there must be a reason
for this, which certainly is not over-netting at the

mouth. To the west there are no bag nets, and to the
east none for some distance. Probably poaching by
the crews of steam-trawlers and the disregard of
the weekly close time by the bag nets are the
causes. I believe it would pay the Naver, Thurso,
Borgie, and Halladale rods to employ a couple of
English keepers each season, who would have
no scruples about visiting the coast nets on
the Sabbath. I am certain they would at first
find plenty of bag nets setting the law and the
weekly close time at defiance; but let the rods
prosecute and prosecute, and listen to no excuses,
and in a short time I believe they would be repaid
handsomely for an outlay which, if shared between
the rods of these rivers, could not come to a very
large sum per head. Two clever men, provided
with good glasses, could also do a good deal
towards watching the movements of the steam
trawlers.

The heaviest fish killed on the Naver weighed
thirty-five-and-a-half pounds, and was taken on the

6th of April, 1891, on Beat No. 6, with a " Warrior,"
by the late Mr. Percy H. Wormald.

In February, 1875, Mr. Alexander Machardy,
fishing the Syre rod on Beat 6, had eight good fish
in one day. Later, two anglers in the spring had
eleven fish in one day. Mr. Pilkington, of Sandside,
fishing the Dalvina rods, had a day of ten grilse and
one salmon on No. 1, and General Lane had eleven
others one day off No. 3. Also in this season of
1899 General Home had five fish on several days.

All these records are, however, not to be compared with the captures made forty years ago by
the late Mr. Ackroyd, who afterwards moved to
Badanloch on the Helm, for he frequently had
twenty spring fish in a day to his own rod. The
following are the takes of the last four years :

1895	.	.	.	.	.	754 fish.
1896	.	.	.	.	.	306 ,,
1897	.	.	.	.	.	364 ,,
1898	.	.	.	.	.	401 ,,

and this season of 1899 will be poorest of all.

John Mackay, the water bailiff, who has been
on the river for over twenty years, thinks that the
severe frost of 1895 did a lot of harm to the ova,
and doubtlessly severe cold, by causing a river
to run very low, leaves many spawning beds to be
frost-bitten and destroyed, though that of itself
would not, I think, be sufficient to cause the falling
off. In the course of a chat with Mackay, he told
me that when he first came to Naver there was a
gentleman of the name of Marshall who labelled all
the kelts he caught, in which operation he was
often helped by a farmer living on the bank; later
on this farmer moved to a holding at Rosehall on
the Cassley, and there he saw an angler land a fish
which had one of Mr. Marshall's marks on it, fully
one hundred and fifty miles from Naver mouth;
and happening later on to revisit Naver, he told
the incident to Mackay.

CHAPTER XX.

THE OYKEL,

WHICH is Gaelic for " The high rising river,"
drains one hundred and thirty-seven square miles,
and is formed by the junction of several small
streams rising at the foot of Ben More in Assynt ;
these expand into Loch Ailsh, and the angling
commences from the outflow of the loch, and
extends for some eighteen miles through the
property of Sir Charles Ross, of Balnagowan, until
the river falls into the head of the Kyle of
Sutherland at Inveroykel. Some dozen miles below
Loch Ailsh are the falls of Oykel, up which fish
are not supposed to go until the middle of May.
The angling immediately above these falls belongs
to the Loubcroy Shootings—" The Horse Shoe
bend "—while those of Ben More have the fishing

rights higher up. After a rainfall sport used to be good on these two stretches of the river, but of late years it has unaccountably fallen off.

OYKEL RIVER AND HOTEL.

Between the falls and the sea there is some seven miles of good fishing, which is divided into two beats and fished alternately by Langwell Lodge and the rod—or two rods—staying at the comfortable

inn at Oykel Bridge. In this interchange of beats
the Sabbath counts as a day, as by so doing the
order of fishing is duly changed each week, for
unless this was done, whoever had Beat No. 1 on
Monday would continue to have it all through the
season.

Wading trousers are wanted. The fish average
ten pounds, though they have been taken up to
twenty-two. Grilse average from three to five
pounds ; sea trout a pound ; and the brown ones
are lanky, black fellows four or five to the pound,
not worth troubling about.

The fly is the only lure permitted ; keepers
and ghillies are only allowed to fish in the
presence of their masters. A landing net must be
used till the 1st of May, but these are served
out to the hotel ghillies, so that there is no need
for an angler to specially provide himself with one,
although the local nets are perhaps hardly made
large enough, or stout enough in the ring, or
sufficiently long and stiff in the pole.

Of the beats below the falls, the upper one is reckoned the best in summer, especially so if it is a wet July — that abomination of the grouse shooter! The lower one offers the best sport in March and April. Though the river opens for net and rod on the 11th of February, closes for nets on 26th of August, and for the rod on 31st of October, quite a fortnight too late, yet there is but little chance of a clean fish before the middle of March, and from that time to the middle of April is the cream of the spring fishing, although as long as there is rain there is always sport to be had.

The top beat includes a couple of good pools on the Einig, a large tributary coming out of the forests of Rhidorrach and Corriemulzie, and joining the main river three-quarters of a mile below Oykel Bridge. The total length of this top beat is nearly three miles ; commencing immediately under the falls there are three pots, short casts in rough water, which in July and August often hold numbers of grilse and sea trout. Shortly below is "George's Pool," so called from a stone on the bank ridiculously resembling the profile of George the Fourth; it is best fished from the left bank, and is rarely without desirable occupants.

This is followed by another pot just above the bridge, while below are four or five likely "bitties," all of them good in summer. Next is "The Washerwoman's Pool," a very good one of some extent, and fishing more or less in any height of water. Below this is the Einig, or Junction Pool, which, as it has a gravel mouth, alters every season according to the severity of the winter floods, and therefore in some years it fishes much better than in others—a troublesome and tricky pool to fish, as there is both slack water and back water at the sides; nevertheless, it is always worth careful casting.

From here the angler on the south bank can turn up to the Fall Pool of the Einig, fishable only in low water, and then come down to the Einig Pool, which is good in medium water; and when in order neither of these beautiful catches should be passed. The drawback of fishing them is the uncertainty as to whether they have not been previously cast over, for the Loubcroy shooting tenant has a right on the west bank, and when there is a good chance, the keeper there is an early bird, so that it is as well to send on the ghillie, and let him find out from the dwellers in a cottage close to these two pools if it has been fished prior to the advent of the Oykel rod.

Returning now to the main stream, about three-quarters of a mile below the Junction Pool comes Big Scorabie, a perfect one to look at, but out of which it is rare to get a fish. The angler on the right bank is advised when making this trip to Big Scorabie not to attempt walking it in wading trousers, for he will have to pass up the "Bad Step," and though the ascent is not a long one, and nothing like so terrible as described by the late Mr. Black in his novel of 'Prince Fortunatus,' it is sharp and steep while it lasts, and those not used to climbing are generally reduced to hands and knees the first time they try it, and once on all fours the small sharp stones quickly cut through the knees of the waders.

The extreme tail of Big Scorabie is sometimes good, and in April, 1896, I hooked and landed three fish from it in as many casts—the only ones taken out of it for many a day.

Next comes Little Scorabie—never without fish, and best worked from the left bank, where the Spey cast comes in handy. At the tail of this the upper beat comes to an end, and the only pools on this section requiring wading trousers are the Junction and the two Scorabies.

Altogether there are seven good pools on this section, and some eight or ten odd corners, and as both banks are included in the beat, there is fair room for two rods in it who are friends, and not jealous of each other.

The lower beat commences at the top of the Long Pool, which in medium water is good at the

head, while in high water the fish lie in the tail.
It fishes from either bank, one side being as
good as the other, but waders are required. Then
comes the Round Pool, a small pot just above a
moderate fall, which also has to be waded. Follow-

LANGWELL LODGE, RIVER OYKEL.

ing this is the Rock Pool, fished from the bank
on both sides, and good in all water, and perhaps
the best on the river. Following this is the
Narrows, a long stretch of easy wading from the
right bank, and every yard of it good. From this

pool in March, 1896, Mrs. Hunt took six fish
one day.   At the tail of this the Stone Pool
commences, which must be waded from the right
bank, but can be fished off the grass from the
left one ; also a very good pool.   A little below
comes Langwell Pool, close to the Lodge, and
my special favourite, for it is a most fascinating
one to fish ; it is deep wading on the right bank,
but is fished from the left off a high, steep cliff,
from which the angler can enjoy the fun of seeing
a fish " come."   At the end of this pool is the
wire suspension bridge connecting Langwell Lodge
with the outside world, and the high road to
Lairg and Loch Inver.   Any angler who has this
lower beat to himself need not bother with going
further down the river, for in March and April the
bulk of the fish .ie between the top of the Rock
Pool and the end of Langwell Pool.   Thus, having
fished one side of this water, it is best to cross and
fish up the other one, and then, if there is sport,
and some of the pools be tried with a couple of

flies, it will take nine hours hard flogging to get over it.

Some half mile below Langwell Bridge comes the Whirlpool, which fishes best, by deep wading, from the right bank, but does not yield many fish. This is followed by the Brae Pool, running under high and nearly precipitous rocks. On the right bank there is only just room to get along, and the Spey cast is necessary to fish it properly. In high water the tail of this is a nearly sure cast; but in low water, though the top of the pool looks splendid, and fish can be seen splashing, it is not often that it gives one. Below this, on the left bank only, there is a long reach of casting from a grass meadow, which at odd times, in high water, yields a fish. This is followed by " The Cemetery," the tail of which in high water is a fairly sure catch, only to be reached from the right bank by very deep wading. Between this and " The Blue Pool " there is about a mile of useless water, and even when " The Blue " is reached it is not of much account.

Then comes "The Turn Pool" (also of no reputation), followed by Inveroykel Pool, a good one in big water, and out of which many more fish would be taken were it not for the long tramp between it and "The Cemetery," for this pool is a tidal one, and it may happen that the angler reaches it when the tide is too high or too low, and so have had his journey for nothing. The pool fishes best from the right bank, and no waders are required.

On the banks of this pool is the prettily placed shooting lodge of the same name, one of Mr. W. E. Gilmour's properties, and usually let each season. From this lodge these lower pools could be more easily and oftener fished, in which case they would doubtlessly show a better yield than at present, for they are but seldom fished by the anglers from above, and it seems a pity they should not go with Inveroykel Lodge.

Grilse begin to run in June, though the chief rush of these lively little fellows is in July. In

1895 the two rods staying at Oykel Bridge Inn got thirty-seven grilse and eighty sea trout in that month. A sixteen-foot rod is ample at any time. and the largest size of fly ever wanted is a No. 3/o Limerick hook ; from that to the very smallest may be used. All the standard patterns kill. Childers and Black Doctor are favourites for morning work ; but Butcher, Jock Scot, Dunkeld, or Benchill are all good. With the two last-named flies in April, 1896, I got twenty-seven fish in as many days. Anyone wishing to know the terms, etc., of the Hotel angling may be sure of an immediate reply by sending a line to the Oykel Bridge Inn.

From the foregoing remarks it will be seen that in the upper beat there is a long tramp from " Junction " to " Scorabie," and on the lower one a still longer journey from " The Cemetery" to " The Blue "; for this reason it is best to start out for the day's work in shoes or boots, except there be deep snow, and let the ghillie carry the waders, and then shift them off and on as occasion requires ;

indeed, on all rivers where trousers are necessary, and the pools some distance apart, it is far more healthy and comfortable to do the walking in shoes, and have the waders carried.

The Oykel, though dependent on rainy weather for sport, is a very pretty river to fish; many of its "bitties" requiring fine and accurate casting. One matter puzzled me very much. During April, 1896, I was every day on the river, and it was impossible not to notice that on each Monday and Tuesday there were always a certain number of clean-run fish to be seen between "The Rock" and "The Langwell"; by Wednesday or by Thursday these fish had all disappeared. Where did they go to? The natives assured me that they do not pass over the falls till the end of April. Had they gathered into the pools below the falls they must have been seen, for the banks are high, and with sunshine and clear water every stone in George's Pool can be inspected. For the same reason these fish also did not pass up the Einig;

there remains only the alternative that they fell back to the salt water of the Kyle, or did ascend the Oykel Falls, the latter being more likely than the former.

The following extract from a letter sent me by Major Burnell Milnes may perhaps support my theory that the fish ascend the falls earlier than is supposed, but for some reason yet to be ascertained they will not then look at a fly. The Major writes: " I have the fishing above the Falls for some six miles of both banks. The sport is about as bad as can be. Both my keepers are very good fishermen and have tried their hardest, and last year (1898) I think one fish was their take. A few years ago a friend went up for a fortnight in June, and though the water was in order, he was blank every day. For some undiscovered reason the fish, when they have got up the Falls, will not take until they get within a mile or two of Loch Ailsh, and there they begin to rise again. Everyone who comes to me in August or

September tries hard at first and thinks he is
going to catch a lot; the water looks nice, you
see fish, and there are any amount of fine pools,
but the result is the same, either a blank day or
a few shy touches."

Chapter XXI.

THE SHIN

Drains two hundred and twenty square miles, and is one of the most beautiful and most sporting of rivers, for though smaller than roaring Awe, it much resembles it in character, as it also empties a big loch and has but a short run to the sea. Loch Shin, from which the river flows at Lairg, is some sixteen miles in length, with an average width of three-quarters of a mile, and consequently the river draining this large reservoir nearly always has some pools in good ply. From the point where it flows out of the loch to where it falls into the Kyle of Sutherland, three miles above Bonar Bridge, the Shin has a run of six miles, in which there is a total fall of two hundred and

seventy feet; quite sufficient to make a rapid
running stream. About four miles below the exit
from the loch is a heavy fall known as "The
Big Falls," which, in spring, is the top pool of
the lower beat, and though it has been opened
up, and fish can very easily ascend, it is rare
for them to make the attempt before the middle
of May; prior to that date all serious salmon
angling is carried on from Mackay's Hotel at
Inveran, renowned for its comfort and pretty site
on the bank of the Cruive or Home Pool.

From the Big Falls to the Kyle the distance
by river is some two miles. Most of the angling
is from the right bank, with the pools nearly
continuous, a short walk or scramble round some
projecting cliff speedily bringing the angler to a
fresh cast.

The birch-clad scenery of the steep rocky banks
is wildly beautiful, so much so that an American
staying at Inveran Hotel recorded in the visitors'
book, "Talk of the scenery of Killiecrankie Pass,

SHIN BRIDGE AND INVERAN HOTEL

why, the Shin licks it into fits!" The river opens,
like the other streams of the Kyle, on the 11th of
February, and can be fished by rod till the 31st of
October, the nets ceasing on the 26th of August.
March and April are the best salmon months, and
June and July for grilse. Clean fish are always in
the water on the opening day, and run from seven
to thirty pounds. The angling is let by the month,
and has been held by the same set of gentlemen
for many years, and except as a sub-let, a rod is
very rarely to be had. From the 11th of February
to the end of March the charge is £82 10*s*., and
all other months are £100, August and September
reckoning as one month.

The fly is the only lure used, the landing-net
being compulsory till the 1st of May, and the hotel
ghillies, John Ross and Hugh Sutherland, are both
supplied with these, and are also both good fly
dressers. The favourite lures are Jock Scot, Black
Doctor—here called the Cromarty—Childers, Blue
and Silver Doctors, and John Ross's invention, "the

Brown Dog "—something like a Childers, and dressed as follows :—

Silver twist yellow floss.

Tail : Topping.

Body : Yellow mohair, picked out; silver tinsel. Half-way up body a claret hackle ending at shoulder.

Wing very spare of black and white turkey bustard, two strands of yellow dyed swan, and sprig of gold pheasant ruff, with topping over all.

Blue chatterer cheeks.

Many of the other standard flies can also be used, the size varying from an iron of three inches down to the smallest double-hooked trout flies, according to the period of the year and weight of water.

As showing how tightly these beats are held on to, it may be mentioned that Dr. H. H. Almond has had February and March for seventeen years, Mr. Lake has held April for nearly as long, and Sir James Ferguson Davie has had May for over thirty years, while Mr. Lewis D. Hall has held the

August and September period for a considerable time.

From the loch to the kyle there are altogether thirty-five named casts and a good few "bitties," and the lower section has the advantage of being fishable without waders. There is just about three hours' smart work from the Big Falls to the sea, so that any fairly hard worker can easily fish the water twice, or even three times, in a day. Quite early in the year the upper pools are not of much account, a state of affairs which is reversed after June, when the lower ones are not productive.

To the friendly kindness of Dr. Almond I am indebted for my first cast and my first fish on the Shin, on the 27th of March, 1896. I fished from the Big Falls to the top of the Cruive Pool without a touch, and then had the luck to land a lively fish of eleven pounds. After this Mr. Almond joined me and fished down the pool again with a three-inch Silver Doctor, which quickly took the fancy of a bright eighteen-pounder, soon to be laid on the bank alongside of mine.

While fishing this pool I was greatly interested in the movements of a hoodie crow and its extraordinary tameness. On pointing this out to John Ross, he told me at this season of the year that particular hoodie did nothing else in life to gain a living beyond watching and waiting on a lot of Mackay's ducks accustomed to paddle about in a reedy bit of river close to the farmyard, and where they were in the habit of nesting. Then, no sooner was an egg laid, than Mr. Hoodie proceeded to discover and devour it. The audacity and trust of this crow had so pleased Mackay that orders had been given to leave it unmolested.

During the months of February and March, 1896, Mr. Almond, without fishing very hard, took sixty-eight salmon, of which a score were twenty pounds or over and the heaviest thirty; the lot averaging sixteen pounds, and between this, his

best season, and a take of but eight in his worst
season, there is a very wide margin. In April
Mr. Lake has varied from twelve to fifty-nine fish
in 1896. Sir James Ferguson Davie in May
ranges from thirty to fifty, averaging eleven
pounds. June gives from twenty to thirty; July
from ten to twenty salmon and from twenty-five
to forty grilse. In August, 1894, Mr. Lewis
D. Hall had nine salmon and twenty-two grilse,
and September gave him six salmon and sixteen
grilse, but from "the twelfth" the rod was often
discarded for the gun. The following are the
takes for the seasons of 1892 to 1899 :—

1892	.	220 salmon	.	. weighed	2900 lb.
"	.	118 grilse	. .	"	645 "
1893	.	101 salmon	. .	"	1150 "
"	.	22 grilse	. .	"	115 "
1894	.	111 salmon	. .	"	1302½ "
"	.	134 grilse	. .	"	741 "
1895	.	168 salmon	. .	"	2155 "
"	.	110 grilse	. .	"	764½ "

1896 .	203 salmon .	. weighed	3101 lb.
,, .	56 grilse . .	,,	330 ,,
1897 .	152 salmon . .	,,	1999 ,,
,, .	88 grilse . .	,,	454 ,,
1898 .	159 salmon . .	,,	2026 ,,
,, .	86 grilse . .	,,	441 ,,
1899 .	108 salmon . .	,,	1380 ,,
,, .	5 grilse . .	,,	23 ,,

Up to end of June.

For many years Lord Braybrooke had the month of July, but in the season of 1889, which was very dry, he did not get a single fish in the whole month, the river being at the lowest point ever remembered, and as the Julys that followed were not much better, his lordship gave up his rod in 1893.

Other successful anglers on the Shin at various times have been Sir Percival Heywood, Sir Archdale Palmer, Colonel Haggard, F. Bibby, H. Gair, I. Usher, and General Gunter.

Sir John Ferguson Davie tells me his acquaintance with the river dates back to 1869, at which period the Little Falls were not blasted, and General Marriott, who then had the angling from the opening to the 1st of May, told Sir James that he had never caught a fish above the Little Fall before the middle of April.

After these falls were blasted fish were got in "Fir Dam," above the Little Falls, at the end of March, and at the present time they are caught even at an earlier date. The heaviest fish Sir James actually landed in his thirty seasons was thirty-two pounds. He has a lively reminiscence of a long fight with a "whopper" on the 24th of May, 1896, hooked in Fir Dam at 12.30 and eventually lost at 7 P.M.—a contest of six-and-a-half hours. This fish only showed himself twice after being "on" for some hours, and on each occasion he rolled over "like a muckle big pig," as old Simon Frazer the ghillie described it.

The best day in May ever had by Sir James was in 1886, when he took eight fish weighing ninety-eight pounds. One day in May, 1883, he had no less than nineteen rises in the day, only seven hooking and all being landed.

Now, from the foregoing statistics of 1892 to 1895, it will be seen the Shin has yielded nine hundred and eighty-four salmon and grilse, or an average of two hundred and forty-six fish each season, and reckoning that as six months, for the first and last few days of the season are not of much use, then the average take per month has been forty-one fish, which does not read very grand sport for the hundred pounds paid. Yet withal, these forty-one fish are well-nigh a certainty, and experienced anglers are quite aware they might go elsewhere, pay more and fare worse, so they stick to the Shin and take the luck of the seasons as they come.

Such a state of affairs, however, may well lead anglers to ask each other why they should not oftener combine together, and by renting nets or paying for an extra twelve or twenty-four hours' weekly close time, double their sport at a small increased cost ? And this I am certain is feasible on many rivers.* In 1898 the Duke of Sutherland sold to Mr. Andrew Carnegie, of Skibo Castle, the angling rights on the Shin from Gruid's Mill to the Kyle, a purchase which created a great flutter of excitement amongst the old rod holders, all of them expecting to get notice to quit ; a pleasant surprise, however, awaited them, and in reply to an enquiry of mine Mr. Carnegie instructed his secretary to write as follows : "Mr. Carnegie desires me to say that he is not rash enough to make any changes in the Shin. Some of the renters have had it for thirty years, and if they were deprived of fishing the Shin, Mr. Carnegie is so enthusiastic a brother of the angle himself as to know that serious consequences might ensue, and he does not wish to have the collapse of any of these fishermen on his guilty conscience."

* See Vol. IV.—Chapter on " Rivers Capable of Improvement."

A very pleasant way of putting matters, for it is not everyone who is a keen angler that would have been so self-denying; Mr. Carnegie, however, is not quite out of touch with his purchase, and has made arrangements by which he can take a cast when he is at Skibo.

In 1897 all the Kyle nets, with the exception of those of Skibo, were rented by my old friend Captain G. W. Hunt, with a view to the immediate improvement of angling, and the ultimate bettering of the netting; ill-health unluckily compelled him to give up in the year following, when fortunately another gentleman, Dr. H. H. Almond, stepped into his shoes with similar good intentions. He writes me: "For the last two years the Bonar nets have been taken off at 6 P.M. on Friday instead of Saturday, or to be even more accurate, they were this year (1898) taken off on Thursdays at 6 P.M. for March and April and fished full time in May. The two upper nets have also been put on later than they used to be, and have been fished very little in August, and as a matter of fact in this season of 1898 they were only on for seven days in August."

The two years taken together, although not showing any profit, have made no loss, and therefore had these nets been rented and worked for profit, the whole of the fish caught in the periods of fishing that were foregone would have been absolutely clear profit, for the men employed were paid the full week's wages, although they worked short time. This season of 1899 these nets are going to be worked full time for four months. One of the Bonar stations is to be left unfished, and it is not intended to fish at all in August; also all grilse from the highest up net are to be returned to the water, and from all the nets the last haul of each tide.

Here, O brother anglers, is something like a tacksman for you! Sad indeed to relate, he has not in all cases met with the support he so richly deserves. Dr. Almond's ideas coincide so closely

with my own that I have asked his permission to
quote *in extenso* an article of his which appeared in
the June number of the *Nineteenth Century* this
year, under the heading: "The Decay in our
Salmon Fisheries and its Remedy." Dr. Almond
writes :—

"This paper will not bristle with statistics.
They are not necessary. The facts with which it
deals are notorious, and the evil for which it pro-
poses a remedy, though not an evil of the first
magnitude, is advancing without any organised
attempt to check it.

"This evil is the decay of our salmon fisheries.

"It is in entire harmony with 'the neglect of
our customers' which has been so trenchantly
exposed in a recent number of this Review.
There is to be seen in both cases the same
flagrant disregard of both principles and experience,
the same complacent fatuous blindness of the so-
called practical man, the same tendency to ascribe
evident decline to fluctuations, to luck, to all causes

except the true one, which is simply want of rationality in both cases.

"It is not too much to say that such blindness, such misconception, and such neglect could scarcely take place in Germany. The school course there, which terminates in the *abiturienten* examination at about the age of nineteen, is a well-organised and thoughtful scheme, which aims chiefly at the cultivation of the reasoning powers. Ours is a haphazard and lawless chaos, and any attempt to construct out of it a training of the intelligence is triumphantly thwarted by a multitude of hetero-geneous and mostly cram-encouraging examinations, as well as by the fallacy which has got a firm grip of the average English mind that information and special accomplishments, rather than the cul-tivation of the understanding, are the proper province of intellectual education.

"Of the latter fact I have been long and pain-fully aware as a schoolmaster; but I have never realised the phlegmatic *vis inertiæ* and unreason of those who are called practical men till a chain of circumstances gave me some acquaintance with salmon, as an article of commerce as well as of sport ; and perhaps this paper, besides its immediate purpose, may also serve to illustrate a matter of far greater importance.

"Various causes have been assigned for the enormous and rapidly increasing decline in the annual output of salmon. For the fact is unquestionable.

"A little reflection will show that it can scarcely be otherwise.

"There are innumerable rights of fishing, existing wherever salmon can be caught—all along the coast, in the estuaries and mouths of rivers, and all the way up the rivers themselves. These rights are subject to the limitation that they may not be exercised during certain weekly and annual close times, and that no fixed engines may be used in rivers or within a defined distance of their mouths. But while the rights are stationary, the efficiency of the engines for taking salmon, and the skill with which these engines are worked, are constantly on the increase, and the fish itself tends to become more valuable from the at least inexpensive nature of the supply. This increased value, again, causes stations to be worked which had previously been unfished— as, for instance, the east coast of Sutherland from the Ord of Caithness to the Fleet, which was unfished by fixed engines till within the last few years.

"There has also been a popular outcry in favour of the 'poor man' catching salmon in the sea, which has been partially responded to by issuing numerous licences in Crown waters, and, I am afraid, a certain amount of condoning unlicensed fishing, by scared or vote-hunting authorities.

"In Ireland I believe that the state of things is very much worse than in Great Britain, and that the salmon is there in imminent danger of being fished out.

"But in this country there is no doubt that

while the close times, the removal of obstructions
on rivers, the hatcheries on some of them, and
more efficient river watching during the spawning
season, have kept us from being brought, except
perhaps on the Solway Firth (where it is wonderful how any salmon ever escapes), within view of
such a catastrophe as this, the annual output is
enormously below what it ought to be, and that
making all allowances for floods, frosts, bad spawning seasons, and other causes, this output is
constantly on the decrease in nearly all parts of
the country.

"The remedy proposed by many, and in which
I once believed myself, is the lengthening of the
weekly close time from thirty-six to sixty hours.
There is no doubt that this would generally have
a beneficial effect, as any one can see who reads
the account of Mr. Archer's experiments in the
Sands district of Norway. But further reflection
shows that such extension of close time would at
once be the signal for upper reaches of rivers

being worked, which, like the Tay above Campsie
Linn, are now not netted because so few fish can
run the gauntlet of the lower nets in thirty-six
hours. To expect that upper proprietors would
refrain from taking an advantage, otherwise than
by improved angling, of such a boon as an increased close time, is not, I fear, in accordance
with experience. Almost every owner of a fishery,
great or small, will grab at every fish which he
can catch without a loss; I believe, in many cases,
even if it were the last salmon.

"Lengthening of the annual close time, again,
which would let more fish up to spawn, is open to
two objections.

"(1) Experts are generally of opinion that some
of each run of salmon and grilse ought to be
allowed to pass rather than all of any one run.

"Without entering into the question whether
spring, summer, and autumn salmon are mainly
different breeds of fish, any one of which can be
improved out of existence, it is pretty certain that

they spawn at different times, so that a great flood or great drought does not affect the whole of the stock of a river, as it would do if all the breeding fish came up and spawned at once.

"(2) This would do nothing for anglers during the greater part of the season. Now I do not wish to make too much of this. All the interests involved — proprietors, tacksmen, labourers, anglers, and the public — ought to be considered. But it is the extreme of narrow-mindedness to lose sight of the facts that many hard brain-workers are by their salmon angling enabled to do better work (personally I can testify to this), and that the presence of anglers on the rivers all through the natural fishing season is an excellent thing in many ways for many of the poorer districts of this country.

"Another remedy is one which, I hear, is now largely adopted in Norway, viz., so increasing the size of the mesh that grilse up to, say, five pounds can get through the nets. The difficulty of arranging compensation to netting lease-holders would be great, if this were done. But, independently of this, I am inclined to believe that the presence of an inordinate proportion of grilse on the spawning beds is in many ways undesirable, and would tend to bring down the size of salmon. I have often wished, however, in the experiences which I am about to detail, that I had felt able to afford trying the experiment of taking off the nets during the grilse season for a year or two. Another serious objection is that sea trout would then escape in multitudes, and these are not only an important article of food and commerce, but are great enemies to the fry of salmon. Still another plan which has been proposed is the prohibition of netting above high-water mark.

"On some rivers, *e.g.* the Tay and Tweed, this would certainly work well. In places like the Kyle of Sutherland, and I believe the Solway Firth, and on some rivers, it would not prevent the decline and perhaps the extinction of salmon.

"The remedy which I am about to propose is

certainly a drastic one, but it seems to me to arise naturally out of the circumstances. Let me briefly recapitulate.

"The salmon is a migratory fish, which, in order to breed, comes in from the open sea, where by methods and in places as yet unknown it has accumulated stores of internal fat. It generally and instinctively makes for the stream where it was bred. It often hits the coast at some distance from this stream, and swims along high and near the shore, so as to be easily caught by bag and stake nets. In the estuaries and rivers these are disallowed, but their place is taken by draught nets, poke nets, hang nets (lately most unfortunately declared to be legal), and other ingenious methods of capture. The rivers themselves may be netted at any point by those who hold netting rights. All these netting rights, on sea, estuary, and river, are exercised without the slightest mutual arrangement or regard to what others are doing. The efficiency of the engines used, the skill with which they are worked, and the pecuniary value of the fish are constantly on the increase. What *can* be the result? The obviousness of the goal to which these causes and circumstances necessarily lead makes one blush for the intelligence of that large part of our fellow-countrymen who have for many years had all the facts before them, and yet have made only fitful and ineffectual signs. As I have told landlords, factors, etc., they will do anything for sheep or grouse, while in regard to salmon they display nothing but masterly inactivity, and talk nonsense about seasons, floods, frosts, sheep draining, and in some districts about the rarely operative *vera causa* of pollution. They see the sheep and grouse, but do not see the salmon.

"What, then, is to be done?

"Clearly there must be combination. And there is no force on earth which will make all these people combine except legislation. Let ever such a good plan be proposed, let it be proved to demonstration that a few years will see netting

produce doubled and angling results more than
doubled by a slight temporary sacrifice, and some
one or two pig-headed individuals (one is often
enough) will block the narrow highway with their
nets. I do not suppose that there is a salmon
district without one or more persons of the class,
who would persistently refuse to put sixpence into
their own pockets if by any chance they would
put sevenpence into a neighbour's.

"I suppose, *e.g.*, that few will deny that there
should be hatcheries on every salmon river. These
do much to prevent the ruin of a spawning season
either by floods at the time of spawning, which
make fish spawn in shallow water, where the
spawn is easily killed by frost, or by droughts at
the spawning season, which make them spawn in
places where the first flood will carry the spawn
away; they are also inaccessible to violent floods
like that of 1892, which sweep away the normal
spawning beds, or (as they can be made frost-
proof) to frosts like that of 1895, which, on many

rivers, froze most of the natural spawn into blocks of ice. They also, under all conditions, cause an enormously greater proportion of the spawn and fry to reach maturity, by protecting them from their numerous enemies. It may here be pointed out that the only two rivers on the north-east coast which have not been rank failures in the recent abnormal spring are the Brora and the Conon, which are also, I believe, the only two on which hatcheries exist.

"But who is to make the hatcheries? The river proprietors would gladly make them (I have a special case in view) if the owners or lessees of the nets at the mouth or along the coast would share the expense, and also let up a fair proportion of each run of fish to the upper waters. But anyone, who has tried to open negotiations with the average tacksman, might as well expect Irish members to combine for the better government of Great Britain, even though they themselves were to be the greatest gainers by it. It would be monstrously unfair to force upper proprietors to do any such thing, unless they have some security that their waters will not be as effectually blocked, during spring and summer, as the bill to prevent the destruction of trout in Scotland was blocked last year.

"Something else must be done first, and then let us have compulsory hatcheries by all means.

"The only true and sufficient remedy is the formation of all proprietors of salmon netting rights in each fishery board district into something like a joint-stock company, each owner of course holding shares in proportion to the value of his fishery.

"The first result of this plan would be an enormous reduction of the number of stations at present worked and of the consequent expenditure. On the Tay twenty stations have been already abandoned by a syndicate which has got most of the river into its hands, and many more would share the same fate if it acquired the whole netting of the river. Some nets, but many fewer than at present, should also be worked in the estuary and on the coast, or the market would be unsupplied in a drought and glutted on the first rain. But the number of the stations is a matter for the experts who would doubtless be employed. I have no doubt that about one-sixth of the present number of stations in the Tay district would at once produce a larger profit, and in a few years an immensely greater profit, than the enormous number which are still worked in it, and that both the output for the public and the value and amount of the angling would be infinitely increased. In the first year or two, of course, the output would be temporarily diminished, because more fish would run the gauntlet of the nets. But the reward for all concerned could not be long in coming. Hatcheries in all districts would automatically be the result of such combination. Where all were pulling together, and not as at present against one another, their value would be too obvious, even to the intellect of the commercial tacksman or the petty proprietor, the genuine *rivalis*, who has more delight in obstructing his neighbour than in populating his own river.

" The objection that this plan would interfere with the rights of property, if compulsion were applied, will not hold.

" For the salmon, being a migratory fish, is not the property of any man till it is caught. And when rights of catching them in any particular place were originally bestowed, the fish were so abundant, and the implements of capture were so rude, that the danger even of serious diminution was not contemplated. Nor can any such right, however bestowed, be allowed to keep down the supply of any valuable food. Indeed, the use of such arguments against compulsion, as are here indicated, is a dangerous *reductio ad absurdum* of the legitimate but essentially limited rights of all kinds of property.

" I believe, however, that legislative compulsion in the background would bring about a certain amount of combination, and many hatcheries as a result.

"But hatcheries without consolidation of fishing stations would do no appreciable good, in many cases, to the upper proprietors, and therefore would not be made. And I greatly fear that in most cases such combination will not take place for the causes which I have indicated above, and which would have seemed to me an incredible instance of human folly and perverseness, had I not been behind the scenes.

"For many years it had been clear to me, as it is to all salmon anglers whom I know, that the stock of salmon is artificially kept far below its maximum. Like others, I once attempted to give evidence on the subject before a Royal Commission, and wrote letters in the *Field* and other papers. But whenever we came into contact with commercial tacksmen, or with proprietors or their representatives, we were accused of speaking in the interest of anglers and against the netting interest.

It was hopeless to prove to minds inaccessible to reason that the interests of anglers, proprietors, tacksmen, and the public were identical, though fishery reports, *passim*, supported our contentions.

"So I determined to become a netter, and to have, if possible, such a large interest in netting as to reduce to absurdity the imputation of being an anglers' advocate.

"The opportunity presented itself on the Kyle of Sutherland and the Dornoch Firth.

"A brief description and narrative are necessary to explain the present state of matters there and its bearing on the general question.

"Dornoch Firth terminates a little below Bonar Bridge in what is called the Kyle of Sutherland. This tidal estuary is about one hundred yards broad at low water for nearly a mile. It then expands for about another mile into the 'Muckle Pool,' then again contracts to a breadth varying from about fifty to a hundred yards, and runs twelve miles further up Strath Oykel, being tidal all that way. Four principal salmon rivers run into it, one of which (the Oykel) afterwards divides into two, the salmon of which are so markedly distinct as to afford sufficient proof, if proof were required, that salmon return to their own rivers.

"The total catchment basin of the Kyle and its rivers is six hundred and twenty-six square miles.

"No fixed engines may be used nearer than Dornoch Church on the north side of the Kyle, or than Inver, some miles east of Tain, on the south side. And, most fortunately, for some miles north of Dornoch Church the nature of the coast is such that fixed engines have never yet been profitably worked. Only a few stations of minor importance are worked along the shore of the Firth by draught nets.

"Up to 1882 the upper part of the Kyle (above Muckle Pool) was so harried by nets that the angling rents were threatened. Fortunately, as one proprietor held these nets and the Shin angling, the most destructive station was closed, and the angling for a year or two bounded up, though two hundred fish (by 'fish' I mean salmon and grilse) were never caught by the rod in the lower beats of the Shin in these years. But about 1884 discoveries in the direction of more efficient methods of netting were made at Bonar Bridge. No records of the netting produce are accessible to me, but the angling take on the Shin fell to ninety-seven fish in 1888 (in which year the upper nets were removed), and to seventy-five in the remarkably dry summer of 1889. But in 1891, for the first time in recent records accessible to me, the angling take on the Shin rose to three hundred and twenty, and in 1892 to three hundred and fifty. The biggest flood of the century, which swept away Bonar Bridge, swept away the spawn, the natural result being that very few grilse were caught in 1893 and few salmon in 1894. Again, things were improving when the big frost of 1895 froze to death spawn and fry. But, in spite of all these drawbacks, in no year since 1890 has the angling take of the Shin fallen below two hundred and forty—a point to which it never rose while the Upper Kyle nets were fished.

" I greatly regret that no records of the netting take at Bonar Bridge are accessible to me. I suspect, however, that, just as the harbour fisheries improved when nets above them were removed, so it must have been at Bonar.

" But I do know that in times long past, with the rude appliances then in use, the annual output of the Kyle and its rivers amounted to well over thirty thousand fish; that, in the opinion of every ghillie, keeper, &c., it gradually declined until the upper nets were removed; that at present, if six thousand five hundred fish are taken on the Kyle net fishings, it pays expenses; and, lastly, that, in the two years of my personal experience, expenditure and revenue have very nearly balanced, though there would have been a moderate profit had the nets been fished full time.

"This experience began in 1897 by a friend, with whom I had often talked the subject over, acquiring all the leases (three in number) at Bonar Bridge, and asking me to join him.* I did so, and circumstances afterwards led to his passing the whole business into my hands, the details, of course, being carried out by a very able professional manager.

"In 1897 and 1898 the nets were removed at 6 P.M. on *Fridays;* one net, which used to go up the Carron River, was taken off (adequate compensation being given by the anglers of that river), and very little fishing took place in March or August. Loss would have been sustained but for subsidies from several of the anglers.

"This year I have acquired three small stations further down the Firth, with the intention of not fishing them, as all fish must pass Bonar. The only other nets at work in the district are a few

* Captain G. W. Hunt.

bag nets at Portnahonnack, near Tarbet Ness, and one small draught net fishing further up the Firth. On the combination principle these should not be worked at all, but the proprietors should have their due share of any profits made at Bonar.

"The wastefulness of all these conflicting stations is sufficiently obvious. And though, if they were consolidated, the total number of fish caught for a year or two would be smaller, the increase to the stock from those which passed Bonar would soon produce a golden harvest. Those taken by anglers constitute, of course, a very small proportion.

"This year, it is as well to say, the nets are to be fished full time for four months. But one of the seven Bonar stations is to be left unfished, and it is not intended to fish at all in August.* It is, of course, idle to predict the precise results of this experiment, but if it does not result in increasing

---

* All grilse also are to be returned to the water from the highest up net, and from all nets the last haul of each tide.

the annual output, all the preceding reasoning will be at fault, and other causes must be sought for the decline of salmon. Personally, however, I feel no anxiety on the subject.

"One or two things have, however, resulted from this partial adoption of the combination principle.

" A considerable number of fry have been presented to the Shin from the Brora hatcheries, and I have reason to believe that a hatchery will soon be established on the Shin, and I hope also on the other rivers. Without co-operation at Bonar this would never have been done.

"The mouth of the Carron is also being made more accessible to salmon, at considerable expense. This, again, would not have been done had the net not been removed from the river.

" I need scarcely add that I hope in a few years to be able to point to indisputable results of the value of 'combination.' I also believe that a continued downward tendency will be evident in all districts which do not more or less adopt it.

" HELY HUTCHINSON ALMOND."

Starting from " The Big Falls," let us now fish the river down.

No. 1. This is a very deep pool, always holding fish from April on, and yields best in medium and low water; when the river is high it is not worth wasting time over. Some five years ago this fall was the scene of a somewhat serio-comic performance —a man from Lairg vanished, and was supposed to have been drowned in the Upper Shin, and on its being suggested that his body would be discovered under the rocky lip of the Falls, the County Council sent for a diver from Wick, who duly found the body and brought it to bank, at the same time reporting to the spectators that there was another one still under the Falls. On being urged to go down again and recover this also the diver peremptorily declined, and, sternly shaking his head, replied, " No, no ; I'm just paid for the one," and getting out of his dress, off he went.

To return, however, to our fishing.

No. 2. " Poll Culag," a deep, rocky pool. Fishing best in medium water.

No. 3. " Cromartie." Has a neck, centre, and tail. Of course in low water it is a case of neck or nothing ; medium water for the centre and high for the tail.

No. 4. " Angus or Round Pool." Is best in lowish water.

No. 5. " The Rocky Cast," the stream above Fir Dam, and only fishes well in very low water.

No. 6. " Fir Dam " is a splendid pool to look at, and excellent when at a medium height.

No. 7. " Clarag " is good all the season through in fairly high water.

No. 8. " The Piper's Pool." Here the river can be crossed by a footbridge of wire.

No. 9. " The Little Falls," divided by a rock in mid-stream into upper and lower ; the latter the best, and requiring a medium water. The upper is best in low water.

No. 10. "The Black Stone" is good all through the season in high water, and fishes well when the river is in such a high flood that hardly another cast is fishable, but it is a case of hold on or break if a hooked fish tries to leave the pool.

No. 11. "Little Clarag." A sure catch in spring in heavy water.

No. 12. "Macpherson's Pool." A made pool, named after a water bailiff, and good in spring with heavy water, when it fishes best from the left bank.

No. 13. "The Turn Pool." A good spring cast.

No. 14. "The Long Pool." Best in low water.

No. 15. "The Parson's Pool." Not nearly as good as it looks. I could not ascertain whether this reputation had any connection with its name.

No. 16. "Smith's Pool" fishes from either bank in high or medium water.

No. 17. "The Artificial Pool," so called from being formed by the construction of jetties. Is good in early spring, and is just above the bridge at Inveran.

No. 18. "The Cruive, or Home Pool," perhaps the best spring cast on the water. It is certainly the longest, and, nearing the tail, quite a lengthy line can be used, and the Spey cast comes handy as the bank behind begins to rise abruptly. From this pool Mr. Almond, in March, 1893, took a fish of thirty-five pounds before breakfast, the largest ever caught in the Shin.

No. 19. "Hector's Land" seldom yields a fish, but is such a pretty pool that it is always a pleasure to fish it, though to the imagination only.

No. 20. "The Garden Pool" is close to the Kyle, and in early spring one of the best for about ten casts towards the tail; but after the end of April it is of no use whatever. Here in March, 1896, Captain G. W. Hunt hooked a fish with a Silver Grey dressed on a two-inch iron, and no sooner did it feel the steel than, with one long, swift, wild rush, it tried to regain salt water. In hot pursuit went the Captain, but being brought to a sudden and painful standstill by getting hung up by the seat of his breeches in a barbed wire fence, the fish broke the line ere his would-be captor could get free. Ten days later John Ross was fishing this pool for Mr. Almond, when he landed a fine fellow of twenty-two pounds with Captain Hunt's Silver Grey still in his mouth.

According to the list of close times published by the Fishery Board, the rod can be plied till the 31st of October; but an understanding has been come to that fishing shall end on this lower beat on the 30th of September. On the upper beat also a somewhat similar arrangement has been made by which the rods stop on the 15th of October, but the whole river should, without doubt, be closed on the 15th of September. On the 1st of September, 1896, I saw five of the blackest, lankiest, and most ugly fish I ever set eyes on taken from a pool a short distance below Lairg. Therefore if they are thus bad at that date, what must they be six weeks later !

We will now take a stroll up the river above the Big Falls, and first comes—

No. 1. "The Boat Pool," which occasionally gives a fish in low water.

No. 2. "The Rock Pool." Also a low water one.

No. 3. "The Long Pool." The best high water catch on this beat.

No. 4. "Grief Pool." Fishes best in low water, and has a sharp ledge of rocks near the tail, amongst which the angler often gets cut, and hence the name.

No. 5. "The Ladies' Pool." Not a great favourite, but gives an occasional fish in high water.

No. 6. "High Rock Pool." A heavy water catch.

No. 7. " Lady Herbert's." A first-rate catch, and fishes best from the left bank.

No. 8. ".The Meadow Pool." A good catch in a June flood, but difficult to follow a fish if it makes down stream.

No. 9. " The Grudie Pool." Pretty good in lowish water. This is the top pool of Mr. Carnegie's water. From here up to the loch belongs to the Duke of Sutherland, and this stretch of two miles is let for June and July to the Lairg Hotel, and from the middle of June on, if there be rain, good sport may be got. Everything depends on the weather, and with that right, the angler should average a fish a day for July. It is very easily fished, and a sixteen-foot rod will cover it all. In August and September Mr. Vernon Watney has the angling for four days of the week with the Tressady shootings, while the remaining two go with the Lairg shootings held by Colonel Stanley Arnold, who also has the whole beat in October. In early September Mr. Watney has had as many as six fish, averaging sixteen pounds in the day, and he also strongly advocates the closing of the river at the end of September.   The following are the pools on this beat :—

No. 10. " The Stream " contains three good

THE STREAM POOL, UPPER SHIN.

casts, and as many as five fish in a day have been had here.

No. 11. " Hector's Pool," a long dull one.

,,   12. " The Lady's Pool " is fairly good.

,,   13. " The Mill Pool," not of much use.

No. 14. " Lord Ellesmere's Pool."

„ 15. " The Tree Pool." Good in medium water.

No. 16. " The Bridge Pool," the highest cast on the river, and close to Loch Shin, used to be very good in high water, but owing to some trees on the bank having been cut down it is now nearly useless. A few yards above this is Loch Shin, in which a few salmon are got each year.

CHAPTER XXII.

THE THURSO.

THIS famous Caithness river, the largest and longest in the county, drains one hundred and sixty-two square miles from its sources in the Knockfin Hills on the Sutherland border to its outfall into the sea at Thurso Bay. For the first twenty miles of its course, until it flows into Loch More, it is little better than a big burn; but on leaving the loch for the final run of twenty-four miles to the sea, it has all the importance of a river. As Loch More is but three hundred and eighteen feet above sea level, there is only an average fall of some thirteen feet per mile, and consequently the bulk of the pools are slow-running ones, called "linns," of almost dead water, only to be fished to the greatest advantage when a steady up-stream breeze ripples their surfaces.

· There are stone bridges at Thurso, Halkirk, and Westerdale, with various wire bridges for anglers, but the river can be crossed in almost any part with stockings, or even in the knee-boots which are mostly affected by the Thurso anglers. Before proceeding further it will be as well to relate a little of the earlier history of the river, which from time immemorial has been famed for the abundance of its salmon. There still exists the certificate vouching for the truth of the largest haul of salmon ever made. It is dated Thurso, August 23, 1792, and is as follows :—

" Mr. George Paterson, now Baillie of Thurso ; George Swanson, shoemaker there ; and Donald Finlayson, senior fisher there, do hereby certify and declare that upon the 23rd day of July, old style, we think in the year 1743 or 1744, there were caught at one haul in the Cruive Pool upon the water above the town of Thurso, two thousand five hundred and sixty salmon. These fish were caught by a large net beginning the sweep at the Cruive, and coming down the stream to a stone at the lower end of the pool. The net was carried down the water by about eighteen or twenty men with long poles in their hands keeping down the ground rope, and the fish were afterwards taken ashore by dozens in a smaller net. Each man got a fish and some whiskey for his trouble. We further personally certify and declare that we were personally present when these fish were caught.—Signed : George Paterson, George Swanson, Duncan D. F. Finlayson."

In more recent years, prior to 1852, these fishings were leased by Messrs. Hogarth, of Aberdeen, who netted Loch More and had the river cross-lined by ghillies, they being paid fourpence a pound for clean fish and keeping all kelts for themselves.

BRAAL CASTLE

Then in 1852 a genius appeared on the scene
in the person of the late John Dunbar, to whom
Sir Tollemache Sinclair gave a long lease of the
river, and later on also built him Braal Castle for
the use of his angling customers. Dunbar was
a favourite with all classes, a keen sportsman,
well up in natural history, and a straightforward,
honourable man; he could likewise enjoy a joke,
and even make one at his own expense, as the
following will show: Having one day to go to
Thurso to appeal against a tax which he thought
he should not have been charged with, the anglers
at Braal teased him by offering to make small bets
that he would not be successful; he accepted them
all, and returned in the evening in high spirits; and
met his tormentors, exclaiming, "Well, gentlemen,
I won my case full easy, for they forgot to pit me
on my o-ath!"

In those early days of the Thurso, the log-book
was not kept with quite the same neatness as it is
now, but even at that date one reads of the doings

of such well-known anglers as the late Lord Lovat,
Sir Francis Sykes, Sir John Blois, Sir W. Gordon
Cumming, and Messrs. A. F. Thistlethwayte, Cor-
rance, Daubuz, Wilson, James Lamont, Francis
Francis, Edmonds, Davidson, and Colonel Priaulx.

Up till 1855 the Thurso flies were dark sombre-
looking lures, but in this year Mr. Meiklam intro-
duced the bright patterns with great success, he
getting with the new lure fifty-six fish in one
week, in which were days of nineteen and thirteen,
and from that time on bright flies became generally
used.

About this date also appeared on the Thurso
Messrs. Frank Enys, Carew, S. Blair, Banbury, Sir
Richard Musgrave, of Edenhall, Colonel Rocke,
Major Traherne, and Captain Warriner. From
1862 the log-book is very well kept, and there
appear the names of Sir Sanford Graham, Admiral
Erskine, Captain H. P. Holford, and Messrs.
Coates, Cunliffe, S. Barker, Adams, and the
Rev. — Meyrick.

The Sunday get-up of the clerical gentleman
afforded many a laugh to the Braal Castle anglers:
a bright-coloured flannel shirt, a threadbare black
swallow-tail dress coat, with a low-cut black vest, old
and very short light-coloured trousers, red cotton
socks, and slippers of green velvet! None the less,
the parson was a "nailer" with his rod, and had
likewise the wisdom to send Captain Holford to
represent him at the kirk. One experience, however, was enough for the Captain, who returned
to relate how the Precentor, no matter whether
sitting down or leading the hymns, kept up an
incessant, noisy, and profuse expectoration, only
varied at intervals by taking huge pinches of snuff
and then blowing his nose with his fingers.

In 1872, Colonel John Hargreaves and his son,
Messrs. J. S. Virtue, Frank Hardcastle, John
Wormald, Sir Henry Boynton, James Wason, and
Lord Kilcoursie are in evidence, followed, in 1877,
by Herbert Grey, R. D. Walker, A. C. Maitland,
and G. Ashley Dodd.

It would perhaps be monotonous to give the take of fish for every year, extraordinary as some of them are, and to save space the records are given in periods of five years.

From 1853 to 1857 :—2,473 fish of 10¼ lbs. average; in 1855 the take was 954.*

From 1858 to 1862 :—3,149 fish, not quite 10 lbs. average; in 1860 the take was 1,041.

From 1863 to 1867 : — 3,570 fish, average 9¾ lbs.; in 1863 the take was 1,510.

From 1868 to 1872 : — 3,084 fish, average 10½ lbs.; and in 1869 it is duly recorded that Mr. S. Barker, being snowed up at Golspie on the 4th of March, walked from there to Braal—fully a fifty mile tramp—his enthusiasm being rewarded later on by the capture of a fine fellow of thirty pounds ; the first ever got on the Thurso.

---

* Until 1857 there were fewer rods, but after that there were seven, and from 1870 there were eight. In 1858 the Loch and Beats 7 and 8 were let separately, and the fish got on them are not included in the log-book.

From 1873 to 1877 : — 3,720 fish, average 11¾ lbs. ; in 1874 the take was 1,240.

From 1878 to 1882 : — 2,392 fish, average 11¾ lbs. ; in 1878 the take was 758.

From 1883 to 1887 : — 2,450 fish, average 11 lbs. ; in 1884 the take was 820.

From 1888 to 1892 : — 2,433 fish, average 11¼ lbs. ; in 1892 the take was 822.

From 1893 to 1897 : — 1,793 fish, average 11½ lbs. ; in 1896 the take was 759; in 1897 the take was 195, which is the smallest ever known.

In 1898 the take was 389 fish, and in 1899 206. This gives a total of 26,379 fish to the rod in forty-seven years, or 561 fish per annum.

During this period there were many great days of sport, the best of which are well worthy of record. On the 9th of May, 1863, Mr. Daubuz had seventeen fish, Mr. Banbury seventeen, Mr. Enys fifteen, and Mr. Edwards six, or fifty-five fish for the day; the two rods on the river being blank. In the same year, on the 11th, the Loch rods had forty-five fish, and from the 24th to the 27th of May Mr. Enys had four successive double figure days, totaling forty-one fish !

In 1864, on the 21st of April, Mr. Enys hooked two fish, one on each fly, on Loch More, and landed them both, the weights being eleven-and-a-half and five-and-a-half pounds.

In 1874, on April 13th, 14th, and 15th, Mr. F. Hardcastle had eleven, seventeen, and thirteen, or forty-one for the three days, the total of the six boats on the 14th being sixty-four fish, and as Lord Kilcoursie had ten on Loch Beg, and the rod on the Linn had two, seventy-eight were taken that day, and the total take for these three wonderful days was a hundred and ninety-two !

On the 27th of April six boats had sixty-four on the Loch, and of these twenty-four went to the rod of Mr. Bayley, while the river rods had only three.

In 1876, the 8th of March, Mr. Enys had three twenty-pounders, and oddly enough a precisely similar day on the 18th of February, 1893 : the only two occasions on which such a record has been made.

In 1892, April 25th, Mr. Ashley Dodd had a fish of thirty-five pounds, and was then just beaten by Mr. Greg a few days later, who had one of

STRATHMORE LODGE.

thirty-six pounds from the Linn on the 5th of May.

In 1894 a most extraordinary state of affairs prevailed, for from the 17th of April till the 14th of May not a fish was got on the Loch.

In 1899, Mr. J. R. Walker, on the 20th of April, had a fish of thirty-five-and-a-half pounds from Loch Beg. This season—the worst but one since 1852—gave a good many big fish, and from a like experience of other small yielding years, it would seem as if the fewer there were the bigger they ran. In 1899, out of the total of two hundred and six, twenty were over twenty pounds. Since 1869 only fifteen fish of thirty pounds or over are recorded; but the yearly weight is nevertheless increasing. In 1863, the one thousand five hundred and ten fish averaged but a fraction over nine pounds, and amongst the lot there were only eight of twenty pounds or over. The present average may be taken at eleven-and-a-half pounds, while many more fish of twenty and over are got each season.

The best takes of single days on the different river beats are as follows, No. 1 being nearest the sea.

No. 1. Seven fish. Mr. F. Enys.

„ 2. Eight fish. Mr. Banbury.

No. 3. Seven fish. Colonel Rocke.

,, 3. Seven fish. Sir R. Musgrave.

,, 4. Eight fish. Mr. F. Enys.

,, 5. Nine fish. Sir Sanford Graham.

,, 6. Ten fish. Mr. Carew.

,, 7. Eight fish. Mr. R. D. Walker.

,, 8. Sixteen fish. Mr. Adams.

,, 9. Ten fish. Lord Kilcoursie. Loch Beg.

,, 10. Twenty-one fish. Mr. Bailey.

,, 10. Nineteen fish. Mr. Wormald.

,, 10. Nineteen fish. Mr. Meiklam.

In 1888, Mr. Dunbar died and Sir Tollemache Sinclair took the river into his own hands; but in 1891 he let it again to a syndicate of six gentlemen, who have held it since. They are Messrs. F. Enys, Herbert Greg, R. D. Walker, J. G. Walker, G. Ashley Dodd, and A. W. Merry. They open Braal Castle on February 1st, and after fishing the river from there until nearly the end of March, they move up to Strathmore Lodge to fish the upper beats and Loch More. It is, however, one

thing to open Braal on the 1st of February, and
another matter to get there, for the Caithness snow-
storms are very severe, as may be seen by the
annexed illustration of the London express, drawn
by three engines, charging a snow block at Altnabraec
Station on the 8th of March, 1895. Up to the
present, the syndicate has not enjoyed any extraordinary good season, their second one of 1892 being
the best, when they had eight hundred and twenty-
two fish. The last three years have been unusually
poor, and average but two hundred and sixty-three
fish a season. I cannot help thinking that this
falling off may perhaps be partly accounted for by
steam trawler poaching, and partly by the fact that
the bag nets to east and west of Thurso mouth
habitually set the law at defiance, and except in
places where the nets are easily approached and
seen, the bulk of them observe no weekly close
time from the day they begin to fish to the day
when they are compelled to stop work. Putting
aside the possibility of any other damaging con-

CHARGING A SNOW DRIFT

tingencies, this of itself must tend to diminish very seriously the supply of fish to the Thurso.

I base my statement on facts previously proved, on my own observations and enquiries, and on the testimony of two friends of mine, who are both of them old anglers and know well what a bag net is. Both were carrying telescopes, and during the course of a Sunday walk in June last from Wick round the coast to Dunnet Head, they could easily see that as soon as they were clear of Wick, every bag net was fishing, though the sea was then, as it had been the previous night, as smooth as a mill pond.

The Thurso Syndicate are also well aware of this lawlessness, and in 1894 they sent two trustworthy strangers to pay a surprise visit to some of the bag nets. At Dunnet Station three were found fishing on Sunday; at Castle Hill Station there were other three. Round Thurso and Scrabster the leads were duly removed, but further off, at Mr. Smith's Station, two nets were fishing. In all they visited

fifteen nets, eight of which were disregarding the
weekly close time.   Six of these were leased by
Messrs. Hogarth, of Aberdeen, who, on being com-
municated with, said it was strictly against orders,
and that men were liable to dismissal and forfeiture
of wages ; that it was a hard law to hold a master
responsible for his servants' actions when the
master's back was turned.   This is, of course,
rubbish, for the law has ever held to the contrary—
a fact which Messrs. Hogarth must have been aware
of.   Needless also to say, that none of the men
were dismissed or lost any of their wages, and I
charge the bulk of the tacksmen with conniving at
this law-breaking and poaching by paying their men
scanty wages and offering them so much extra per
head per fish caught, which is tantamount to directly
bribing them to break the law.*

I really think this incessant bag-net fishing must
have something to do with the fall off of the

* See Vol. II., Chapter on " Netting—Legal and Illegal."

Thurso take, and believe it would pay the syndicate
to make five or six such surprise visits each season,
and to call public attention to all cases of detection,
and to press such to a conviction. Needless to say,
the persons chosen for the business must be strangers,
and the same two should not be employed twice ;
but on this and the other matters connected there-
with the syndicate probably know more than I do.
Setting aside the risk of a spring snow block, the
Thurso is easily reached nowadays, for one can
leave Euston at 8.50 in the evening and dine at
Braal or Strathmore the next day. In 1869 the
limited mail from Euston did not reach Golspie till
6.30 the next evening, or some seven hours later
than it does now, and this meant sleeping another
night on the road.

With the exception of three miles on the right
bank below Westerdale and about five on the left
bank, the whole of the Thurso belongs to Sir
J. G. Tollemache Sinclair, and though on these
odd miles that are not his the respective owners

have the right of using a net coble, it has been decided by law that this method of fishing does not also carry with it the right of angling with a rod.

The river is an early one, opening on the 11th of January, and closing on the 14th of September. The nets immediately round the mouth are rented by the syndicate, and are not worked. From the 1st of April to the middle of May is the cream of the angling; but at times continuous high winds so stir up the loch as to make it muddy, and when once in this state it remains dirty for a considerable time. Grilse begin to run about the end of May, and of these more can be taken with a trout fly than with anything larger. To fish the river with comfort three rods are required —one of eighteen feet for the spring, one of sixteen feet for the river from the end of April, and one of fourteen feet for the loch. The *short*, heavy double taper line invented by Mr. Greg is an excellent one, for it will send out a big fly in the

teeth of a high wind, or send a small one lightly
and truly to the end of an extra long cast of fine
salmon gut.   Both in the slack pools of the river
and in the loch, fish are apt to take just as the
fly is being lifted, and there are more rods broken
here than on any other dozen rivers in Scotland.
There is a story of a novice guest who, as one
of the old hands ruthlessly put it, "could not throw
a fly as far as a good Yankee could spit."   He
arrived with half-a-dozen rods, and three days later
he wired his tackle - maker, "Send me a dozen
salmon rods by return!"   There is no compulsion
to carry a net.   The gaff is used, it being understood that kelts are to be hand-lined, lifted from
the water, and returned uninjured.   As to the
Thurso flies, there are no such things as standard
patterns; ranging from irons four-and-a-half inches
long to the very smallest, any bright-coloured combination of mohair, tinsel, hackles and feathers will
kill. The more yellow the better, as the water
often is peat-stained, and then that colour shows

more conspicuously than any other. Here is the dressing of two old flies that lie before me as I write, and each has seen service. The first is an excellently well-tied one of Mr. Enys'—a nameless creature, which might well be christened the Enys, for that gentleman holds the honour of being father of the river.

Iron three inches long.

Tail: Red ibis, or dyed swan; one-third of body gold twist, two toucan feathers, and a red but at the top of this; the remainder of body equal lengths of yellow and blue mohair with broad silver tinsel; a claret hackle with blue over it, and a gallina over that; all three at shoulder.

Wing: Long strips of brown turkey feather with red and blue macaw, covered with three jungle cock feathers on either side, arranged so as to form a happy sequence.

The other fly was tied by Colonel Rock and is simply a sort of "canary"; on an iron the same size as above.

Tail: Red ibis.

Body: Bright yellow mohair; silver tinsel and mohair picked out between the turns in an ascending scale; a yellow parrot hackle at shoulder, and the wing strips of bright yellow dyed swan, with two strands of red macaw over all.

This fly will kill in highly-coloured water in other rivers than the Thurso, for I put it on one day when fishing the lower Careysville water of the Blackwater in Ireland, and quickly got five fish with it.

To the fly tieing amateur, therefore, the Thurso offers an endless field for inventions, but for February and March "big and bright" are the passwords to success. Any lure may be used, but the fly is the best, for those trying bait continuously have ever been the least successful. From the 1st of July, however, when the angling goes with the shootings of Strathmore and Braal Castle, no other lure than the fly is allowed.

At present the river is divided into eight beats,

so that each rod has a daily beat on the loch as
well as one on the river. Beats Nos. 1 and 2,
nearest to the sea, are seldom fished after February. The weather cannot be too mild for the early
fish, and is more often than not a great deal too

LOCH MORE.

severe for sport. Each beat holds plenty of fishing,
and No. 7 is the most sporting of the lot. It
begins some mile and a half below Strathmore
Lodge, and from its starting-point at "The Old
Woman's Pool," "The Sauce Pool," "Maggie

Stumpie," " Bridge Pool," " Long Pool," " Castle Pool," and " Devil's Pool," which is about half the beat, are all fine quick-running casts with very little, if any, dead water.   The syndicate use fish-shaped wicker baskets for packing, procured from the Blind Institute at Hull, which are excellent for the purpose, and I venture to hope some of my readers may give them a trial, for they will do themselves and the Charity a good turn ; they are cheaper than boxes, and are very quickly fastened up.

Loch More begins to be good about the end of March ; it is a small circular shallow loch of some two miles in circumference, and about a quarter of an hour's drive from Strathmore Lodge. In taking what I trust may be only a paper leave of the Thurso—for I hope yet to see it once more—I must tender my best thanks to my friend, Frank Enys, for his kind help, and I am sure the rest of the syndicate will join with me in wishing him many tight lines for many years to come.

CHAPTER XXIII.

SOME REMARKS ON DR. NOEL PATON'S "INVESTIGA-
TIONS ON THE LIFE HISTORY OF SALMON," ON
MARKING, AND ON HATCHERIES.

THESE investigations, published with the 1898
Report of the Fishery Board, are regarded by
their author as finally settling the question as to
whether salmon feed in fresh water. The Doctor
does not make a very happy start by telling his
readers "that in spite of the most careful study
by scientific investigators, the migrations of the
salmon, and the various changes in condition
which it undergoes, are even now far from being
understood." Up to this point, probably, everyone
will agree with him; but there are many who will
be ready to differ with him when he continues—

"and the careless observations and foolish traditions of keepers and ghillies have only served
to involve the matter in a deeper cloud of
mystery."

It would have been interesting to have been
told in what parts of Scotland Dr. Paton met
with these careless observers, and foolish, mys-
terious traditionists; also it would have been as
well if he had defined the nature and character
of the alleged stupidities. For forty years I have
talked fish with numerous keepers and ghillies,
and fail to recall to mind any flagrant instances
of careless observation or belief in any absurd
traditions of salmon life.

On the contrary, I have found both keepers
and ghillies well informed as to all the ordinary
habits of the salmon in the particular river which
they were employed to preserve. Of course they
were not possessed of that scientific knowledge
which is the privilege of the few, but nevertheless
they were well acquainted with all the incidents

of salmon life, most of them knowing quite as much as their employers.

Now if the Doctor approached the rivers he visited (he does not name them) with the feeling that all the keepers and ghillies were fools, then I am sure they would at any rate be sharp enough to detect that sentiment, and so become hostile and unwilling to render him help.

Dr. Noel Paton next proceeds to demonstrate, well and clearly, that from the moment a salmon enters fresh water every organ in its body commences to undergo a change, while even some of the substances of the body shift their position from one part to another. He tells us how, in April or May, the ovaries of a hen fish constitute but 1·2 per cent. of her weight, while in November the same organs are 23·3 per cent. of her weight, a fact on which the Doctor lays very great stress. But surely there is nothing new or remarkable in telling us that the longer an animal carries its young the greater will be the weight of the organs concerned, and the eggs of a salmon are its young and increase in size, and consequently in weight, until they are ready to be deposited on the river bed.

The Doctor then mentions how curious it is that food should be found in so small a percentage of the fish captured at the mouths of rivers, and reminds us that the estuary is not the natural feeding ground, and therefore it is probable that only by chance are any traces of food discovered in estuary-captured fish, although in the deep sea it is well known salmon feed on herrings, haddocks, whiting, sand-eels, sand-worms, shrimps, sand-hoppers, and various other crustacea : all these having been found in the stomachs of salmon caught in the sea.

We next learn that the stomachs of salmon entering a river at the commencement of their fast present marked and striking differences to the stomachs of those that have been for some time in fresh water, while the stomachs of kelts begin to regain the normal appearance as soon as spawning is over. The Doctor then relates how, in November, he netted a number of fish from the upper reaches of a river, and, on examination, he found the gall bladder was quite collapsed, while in the fish taken from the estuary at the same time, and in nearly all the kelts, the gall bladder was distended and ready to help in digestion.

This degeneration of the alimentary tract during the stay of the salmon in the river is therefore accepted as proof positive that no absorption of food is possible.

In May and June the difference in the weight of fish captured at the river mouth, and of those taken in the upper waters, is practically *nil;* but in July and August the fish of the estuary are nineteen per cent. heavier than those of the upper water, which is but a scientific corroboration of the fact, already well known to all anglers, that spring fish lose weight during their stay in fresh water.

Dr. Paton is, I believe, quite right in ridiculing the theory that very early-run fish turn back to the sea. His investigation goes far to explode this idea, for, as he says, " if there were a constant to-and-fro migration from river to sea, and from sea to river, we should not expect to have discovered those strongly marked differences between the estuary fish and those of the upper waters."

Miescher Reusch, the German scientist, who examined two thousand Rhine fish taken at Basle, five hundred miles from the sea, found nothing in the stomachs of one thousand nine hundred and ninety-eight of them, the two exceptions being the stomachs of two kelts, in which there appeared undoubted traces of feeding. Reusch further states that between the 20th of May and the 12th of October the Rhine fish lose six per cent. of their weight, which is a smaller loss than is looked for by anglers at home ; for, according to this calculation, a May fish of fifty pounds would still be forty-seven pounds in October ; but surely forty-four pounds, or even less, would be nearer the mark. In ascending a river a salmon has not only to raise its weight to a given height, but it also has to overcome the friction of the stream, so that in a river with a rise from the sea to its upper spawning beds, say of seven hundred feet, a fish will have to lift its weight up that height, while in addition it will have to overcome the force of the various streams which it has to ascend, a matter requiring a still greater expenditure of strength, and the total tax thus imposed must be severe.

Then Dr. Paton tells us that the beautiful pink colour of the flesh of the fresh-run fish is derived from a pigment, which, as it ascends the river, passes slowly from the flesh of the female into the ovaries, turning them a brilliant orange-red, the flesh meanwhile becoming paler and paler until spawning is over and the sea about to be revisited. In the male this pigment or colouring matter of the flesh is transferred to the skin, and hence that red-copper colour the cock fish assumes before spawning.

As to whether salmon feed in fresh water, those who maintain they do are quite as right as those who say they do not! Everything depends on what is understood by "feeding." Those who contend they feed say that this means the act of swallowing either flies—real or artificial—insects, worms, minnows, prawns, etc. Those who say salmon do not feed in fresh water, maintain that feeding does not mean the mere swallowing of material, but further implies digestion, absorption, and utilisation by the body of the material swallowed ; and the fact that salmon do take down some of the above-mentioned luxuries is not argument as to their feeding in this sense. They admit a fish will swallow a big bunch of lob worms right into his stomach (on the Dee I have watched plenty of clean fish take from thirty to fifty March Browns one after the other as long as the rise lasted, and this several times a day) ; but it by no means follows that they are digested or used to form flesh, or muscle, or fat. Certainly, this theory makes our dear friend, Mr. Salmon, look a bit of a fool, and as if he did not know what was good for him! In this respect, however, he is no worse off than those of his two-legged friends on the bank, who know they cannot digest nuts and port wine, and yet take them!

Dr. Paton, in order to help the unscientific mind to realise the possibility of a fast "for several months" in such an active, hard-working creature as the salmon, brings forward the case of the male fur seal, who, when coming ashore for fighting and love-making, is "said" to go for over a hundred days without food, while even warm-blooded animals are known to undergo prolonged fasts during the rutting season. A fast of over three months for so big and fat an animal as the fur seal may be possible, but it will be noticed that his case is only described as "re-ported," and not as an ascertained fact. In the

case of the salmon, Dr. Noel Paton's "several
months" of fasting may often extend to the best
part of a whole year ; and it is difficult to realise
that such a prolonged abstinence can be possible.

Take the case of a fish coming into the Spey
in February. By easy stages it pushes its way up
to Loch Insh, and then again, proceeding onwards,
let us suppose it turns into the Tromie, and, con-
tinuing the forward movement, it eventually ceases
its travels as it nears Loch-an-Seilig, in Gaick Forest.
By this time it will be the end of May, and there,
in the Tromie river, the foresters will see this particular fish almost daily, until, in September or
October, it finds a mate, spawns in November, and
takes its departure from its home in the Tromie
some time in December. How long it requires to
again reach the sea is a matter of conjecture, but
the distance must be something like eighty miles.
Here then, at any rate, is a fish who has for
certain been in fresh water from February to
December—ten whole months !—and, according to

Dr. Paton, during the whole of that period it will not have eaten anything it could digest, or from which it could derive any benefit, and in such a prolonged fast I, for one, cannot believe.

Take, again, the Tay and Loch Tay. At the opening day, on the 15th of January, there are always fresh-run fish in the loch, which certainly do not spawn till November, or turn seawards till December, another case of a fast of ten or eleven months, which is considerably more than one of "several months," and, with all due deference to Dr. Noel Paton, I venture to think this question of feeding in fresh water is not so absolutely settled as he considers it. He concludes by relating a curious incident with regard to the downward migration of kelts. In April, 1897, twenty-two of these were sent him for dissection (he does not say from what river or rivers), and as the whole of them were hens, he naturally asks, "Is this a mere coincidence, or do the male kelts descend at a different time from the females?"

I cannot but think the matter was chance, for
in the lower reaches of the Dee I have landed
upwards of a thousand kelts in March and April, and
amongst them were about as many hens as cocks.
The question is, however, one which the head man
of any river nets could easily settle, for great
numbers of descending kelts must come into his
nets and under his notice each season. With
regard to this catch of kelts by net and by rod,
it has always seemed to me a regretable matter that
the chance thus offered of marking larger numbers
of fish has not been better utilised, for if there is
anything to be learnt by marking fish, it should be
done by thousands and not by hundreds. In the
same way it would be instructive if a large number
of clean fish could be netted in the weekly close
time, and returned to the river duly marked—a
breach of the law for which, in the cause of science,
permission could doubtlessly be obtained. On the
Aaensira and Sands Rivers of Norway, Mr. Archer
has marked large numbers of kelts, a fair proportion

of which were caught again as clean fish either in the respective rivers they belonged to, or so close to their mouths as to leave no room for doubt that, had they escaped the nets, they would have returned to the rivers they had been bred in. On the other hand, a good many of these marked fish were taken by bag nets stationed from one to five hundred miles distant, which would make it appear as if the salmon took very long journeys during its stay in the sea; and the fact that bag nets placed many miles away from the mouth of any river often take great hauls, certainly makes it look as if the fish swam for long distances along the shore in search of their respective rivers.

With regard to the establishment of hatcheries, there is some difference of opinion as to their usefulness; but where the return of fry made to the river nearly equals the number of eggs taken from it, then surely that must in the long run far exceed any natural yield, for in a hatchery, floods, frosts, and droughts are powerless to destroy the ova, while the eggs themselves are protected from the ravages of fish or birds. If, moreover, the burn into which the fry are eventually turned be previously dammed back until the bed is nearly dry, and all trout and eels carefully removed, and if it be further protected by fine netting or perforated wire from the overhead attacks of gulls, etc., then it can safely be asserted that the artificial method will be much more productive than the natural one.

Of course there must come a period when the fry has to be turned into the river, and once there they will have to take their chance with their nature - hatched brethren ; and I have met with people who maintain that the artificially reared fry are not so sharp as the natural bred ones in protecting themselves from the attacks of gulls, etc. ; that the river-bred fry will instantly seek shelter under stones at the sight of a gull overhead, while the artificially reared ones will not recognise the foe until too late.

Many hatcheries are kept up by private

gentlemen, as, for instance, those of Lord Abinger, on the Spean, the Marquis of Ailsa's at Culzean, Lord Breadalbane's at Taymount, Lord Burton's at Glenquoich, Sir John Fowler's at Braemore, Mr. Pilkington's at Sandside, the Duke of Richmond's at Fochabers, and the Duke of Sutherland's at Torrish, on the Helmsdale. This latter hatchery I had the advantage of seeing, under the guidance of Mr. Macfarlan and his keeper, Mackay, who superintends it. There are others at Alness, Brora, Conon Bridge, Dupplin, Durris, Howietown, Loch Buie, Stormontfield, Tongueland on the Kirkcudbrightshire Dee, and last, but not least, that of Mr. Armistead, on the Solway. Some of these hatcheries belong to the District Fishery Boards, and others to those who breed to sell. In a few places hatcheries have been abandoned, but this has been chiefly owing to bad management; and, as a rule, when they have once been started, they have been maintained on account of benefits received.

The following rivers are not provided with

hatcheries, and I quite believe that all of them would be improved if they were properly started : Annan, Awe, Ayr, Cassley, Carron, Cree, Dee (Kirkcudbrightshire), Deveron, North Esk, South Esk, Findhorn, Forth, Ness, Nairn, Oykel, and Shin.

If there is any good at all in hatcheries, each first-class river should have at least two large ones, and the District Boards should have power to order their erection and be able to provide for their cost and maintenance by a *pro rata* tax on every one deriving profit or sport from the river or its coast fishings.

In the United States and Canada, hatcheries have been most successfully established and maintained by Government. Now, in Scotland we have been legislating for salmon for some hundreds of years, but up to the present the State has done nothing to help artificial propagation. In the United States there is a completely organised government department for the purpose of breeding fish artificially in order to increase the stock in the rivers and lakes, and likewise to supply fry to those waters in which fish once existed, and where they have become extinct from pollutions, obstructions, over-netting, or any other cause. The Americans say that Great Britain protects fish (*very, very* badly, I say!) and does not breed them; the United States breeds fish and does not protect them. How successful the Americans have been may be judged by the following extract from a letter written by Professor Baird, of Washington, to the Commissioner of Fisheries for Canada. He says :—

"In the Sacramento River we are absolutely certain of our ground, having brought up the supply of salmon to more than its pristine condition of abundance by planting about two million of young fish every year. The catch there has increased in five years from five million to fifteen million pounds, and in 1881 there was more fish than could be utilised in all the canning establishments on the river. No one questions in the remotest degree the thorough efficiency and success of the artificial work." I believe, however, that there are not the enormous numbers of bag nets on the American coasts as there are on those of Scotland, and that without a curtailment of their numbers and a setting of them back from the mouths of rivers, and without a vigorous enforcement of the weekly close time and a lengthening of it, that the establishment of Government hatcheries, though they might slightly benefit the river proprietors, would yet increase the profits of the owners and lessees of the bag nets in a much greater degree. And in this country it may be taken for granted, as long as the present system of coast nets continues to exist, that hatcheries will not do everything that is required to restore our salmon fisheries; but they would go a long way to this end if backed up by better protection against poaching, by the prevention of netting in the weekly close time, and by judicious alterations of the estuary lines. So unfair are the hardships and wrongs inflicted on the river proprietors by the already enormous and yet steadily increasing numbers of the fixed engines, and so continuous and so clearly marked is the falling off in the salmon supply, that the day cannot be far distant when Parliament will be compelled to take these matters in hand in earnest, and by fresh legislation bring both salmon eating and salmon angling within the reach of the masses.

END OF VOLUME I.

Lightning Source UK Ltd.
Milton Keynes UK
UKHW011041210519
343056UK00007B/2265/P